ARCHITECTURAL DESIGN

EDITORIAL OFFICES:
42 LEINSTER GARDENS, LONDON W2 3AN
TEL: + 44 171 262 5097 FAX: + 44 171 262 5093

EDITOR: Maggie Toy
DEPUTY EDITOR: Ellie Duffy
DESIGN: Mario Bettella and Andrea Bettella/Artmedia

CONSULTANTS: Catherine Cooke, Terry Farrell, Kenneth Frampton, Charles Jencks, Heinrich Klotz, Leon Krier, Robert Maxwell, Demetri Porphyrios, Kenneth Powell, Colin Rowe, Derek Walker

SUBSCRIPTION OFFICES:

UK: JOHN WILEY & SONS LTD
JOURNALS ADMINISTRATION DEPARTMENT
1 OAKLANDS WAY, BOGNOR REGIS
WEST SUSSEX, PO22 9SA, UK
TEL: 01243 843272 FAX: 01243 843232
E-mail: cs-journals@wiley.co.uk

USA AND CANADA:
JOHN WILEY & SONS, INC
JOURNALS ADMINISTRATION DEPARTMENT
605 THIRD AVENUE
NEW YORK, NY 10158
TEL: + 1 212 850 6645 FAX: + 1 212 850 6021
CABLE JONWILE TELEX: 12-7063
E-mail: subinfo@wiley.com

ANNUAL SUBSCRIPTION RATES 1998: UK £90.00, student rate: £65.00; Outside UK US$145.00, student rate: $105.00. AD is published six times a year. Prices are for six issues and include postage and handling charges. Periodicals postage paid at Jamaica, NY 11431. Air freight and mailing in the USA by Publications Expediting Services Inc, 200 Meacham Ave, Elmont, Long Island, NY 11003.

SINGLE ISSUES: UK £18.99; Outside UK $29.95. Order two or more titles and postage is free. For orders of one title please add £2.00/$5.00. To receive order by air please add £5.50/$10.00.

POSTMASTER: send address changes to AD, c/o Publications Expediting Services Inc, 200 Meacham Ave, Elmont, Long Island, NY 11003.

Printed in Italy. All prices are subject to change without notice.
[ISSN: 0003-8504]

CONTENTS

ARCHITECTURAL DESIGN MAGAZINE

Jyrki Tasa, House Into, Finland

ARCHITECTURAL DESIGN PROFILE NO 133

HYPERSURFACE ARCHITECTURE

Stephen Perrella *Hypersurface Theory: Architecture><Culture* • **Brian Massumi** *Sensing the Virtual, Building the Insensible* • **Michael Speaks** *It's out There . . . the Formal Limits of the American Avant-Garde* • **Gary Genosko** *The Acceleration of Transversality in the Middle* • **Mark Burry** *Gaudí, Teratology and Kinship* • **Reiser + Umemoto** *Yokohama Port Terminal* • **Lars Spuybroek** *Motor Geometry* • **Kas Oosterhuis** *Salt Water Live* • **Studio Asymptote** *Architexturing Copenhagen* • **Bernard Cache/ Objectile** *Topological Architecture and the Ambiguous Sign* • **Van Berkel & Bos** *Real Space in Quick Times Pavilion* • **Claude Parent** *The Oblique Function meets Electronic Media* • **Stephen Perrella** *with* **Dennis Pang/Rebecca Carpenter** *The Haptic Horizon* • *The Möbius House Study* • **Marcos Novak** *Transarchitectures and Hypersurfaces: Operations of Transmodernity* • **Coop Himmelb(l)au** *UFA Cinema Centre, Dresden*

Kas Oosterhuis, Salt Water Pavilion, The Netherlands

Marcos Novak, Warp Map

JYRKI TASA
HOUSE INTO
Espoo, Finland

This house has been designed as a one-person residence that can provide good conditions for social life. Emphasis is placed on the living room and social space, while the bedroom areas and service space are comparatively small. The aim is to create an unprejudiced and modern design utilising the beauty and softness of wood and the elegance and elasticity of steel. House Into was completed in 1997.

The building site is located on a high, west-facing hill: a position that enables the structure to open up to the evening sun and to the sea. The approach is from the south, towards the white curved wall of the building. This element provides shelter while discreetly shielding the view of close neighbours. The curved eaves and long, slanting steel columns of the west side are only partly visible when

approaching a small bridge crossing a water basin to the main entrance.

On entering the house, a view of the terrace and the sea opens up through a high glass wall. At the same time, an impression of the design is created by the high entrance and stair hall at the centre of the building, which connect one space to another both spatially and functionally.

The bedrooms are located to the left and the sauna and swimming pool to the right. The living room and the kitchen are situated upstairs, each with balconies that exploit the afternoon and morning sun respectively. The ground floor, which can be seen from the entrance hall, contains the hobby and service areas and the exit to the garage which is situated beneath the terrace.

Several vertical architectonic elements

are connected to the central hall area. The stairs make use of plywood folded plate, supported by steel wire structures suspended from the ceiling. A white, reinforced-concrete tower contains three smokestacks and two fireplaces which open up to the swimming pool and the living room.

The tower rises 12.9 metres from the lowest level up through an oval rooflight, culminating in three steel smokestacks. In the entrance hall, one of the walls is made of glass bricks, enabling light to be filtered to the stair hall from the living room, bathrooms and hobby room on the ground floor.

House Into is constructed principally of wood and steel. The external walls are covered by boards and plywood, and those of the interior mainly covered by pine plywood.

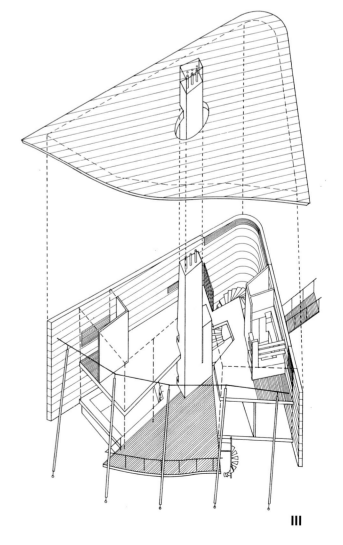

RIGHT: Cutaway isometric

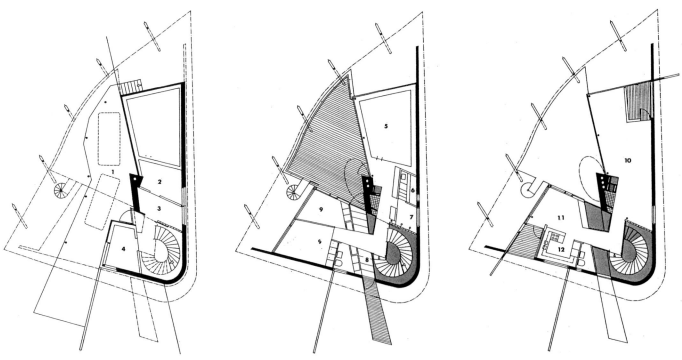

IV

OPPOSITE, L TO R: Ground-floor plan;
first-floor plan; second-floor plan

TRELLICK TOWER
BREATHING IN AND BREATHING OUT
Max Baring

American artist Allan Kaprow once famously declared that 'the daily traffic jams on the Long Island Expressway are more useful than Beethoven, Racine, or Michelangelo'. Kaprow was one of the pioneers to move art out of the studio and gallery and into the real world. For the last 20 years Ron Haselden has been following his lead. Trained as a sculptor, Haselden soon found himself frustrated by the limitations of traditional sculpture. 'I felt very strongly that sculpture was clutter. Sculpture as an object became an obstacle rather than a liberating force.'

Two years ago the architect Robert Barnes was commissioned to design new business units alongside the railway lines opposite the Trellick Tower in West London. 'We designed a very low two-storey building which was 100 metres long, and here we were building opposite the Trellick Tower, one of the icons of 20th-century housing design, which is 100 metres high. I felt there was a relationship between the two pieces of architecture that could be brought out by a major public art event'. The two buildings are separated only by the busy railway lines which lead in and out of Paddington Station.

Barnes called on Haselden to collaborate on a trio of grand scale lightworks entitled 'Breathing In and Breathing Out'. On a Friday evening last November, the first of a trilogy of public arts performances took place at Erno Goldfinger's famous tower block. This first installation involved an interaction between several elements: the tower block and its inhabitants, the passing trains and the new offices opposite. Each resident on one side of the 29-storey Trellick Tower was provided with a 500-watt lamp and a set of six coloured gels.

At the business unit on the other side of the tracks, a large number-board made of fluorescent tubes was erected. Each time a train passed the number board was triggered and advanced so that after 40 minutes the board had counted up from one to 30. Each resident was given a unique sequential script. This denoted the colour of gel for the light on their balcony for each numbered stage. By changing from one gel to another each resident was playing their part in creating the overall changing patterns which were to decorate the front of the block.

It was important for both of the creators that this was not seen as a slick sequence that you might find in a large airline or bank advertisement. As Haselden points out: 'It is the unexpected human factor that is of a lot of interest to me; sort of anti-technology in a way so it brings us back to ourselves to look at. Were not sure how its going to look. We've had no rehearsal as that would destroy the nature of the work'.

Different people had different roles and reactions. Some residents either chose not to, or couldn't turn up to operate the lights from their balconies. On a blustery night, nature even took a hand, blowing one tenant's gels off her balcony. One father got someone else to man his light for him so that he and his young son could join the crowd below and watch the spectacle. What if the phone rang in one flat? Would a colour change be delayed?

People got confused with their gels and put the wrong one on. It is as if the formal process was set up to fail, and these failures generated the character of the piece contributing to its success. Every glitch, gap and anomaly expressed something of the nature of life in the tower, and the observer could muse on the variations thrown up by the performance. 'The sculpture relies a lot on the unpredictable happening,' observed Haselden.

The trilogy is an interaction between the architecture, the occupants of the buildings, London's communication networks and the artwork itself. The work operates at the level of the whole building, the level of individual corridors, of separate flats, but also at the much wider level of the whole of West London. The tower is visible from Richmond Hill seven miles to the South, and all the way along Marylebone Road two miles to the East.

The work was rooted in the community in additional ways. The designs for the facade were based on children's drawings from a local school, and patterns generated by the Moroccan Women's Centre that meets weekly in the club room in the tower block. As Barnes observes, 'Ron is incredibly unprotective of his work, it is so inclusive that the performers really get to feel involved'. This is borne out by Martin Kingsford, Chief Executive of Council Housing in the Borough. 'I have worked on Trellick for 17 years. I sensed a feeling of real pride by the residents of Trellick, a real sense of participation and ownership which the art form was able to give. The like of which I have never before experienced'.

Perhaps the inclusiveness is due to the light-hearted nature of the work, suffused as it is with a delightful sense of humour. It also has something to do with the simplicity and literalness of the materials, and their straightforward use. On the night, with 30 minutes to go, the number board is playing up. One of the fluorescent tubes won't turn off and a 3 looks like a 9. Finally, the electrician gives the sequencer box a firm kick and the board corrects itself; 'That should do it'. Haselden sums it up: 'Light is a vulnerable medium. There's a kind of fragility about it that materials like bronze and stone never seem to have. For all the technological advances, it's still open to disaster. It may not work on the night. It has that tension about it'. The formation of the structure is reinforced through the gaps that appear in the performance.

The second and third parts of the trilogy of lightworks will appear this year. The second piece is intended to last a year. It plays with the free-standing lift-shaft, and the passage-ways linking the shaft to every third storey of the tower block. Sensors pick up the tenants moving about the building and express their movement in lights on the outside of the concrete structure.

The final installation will be sited on the new long, low building units facing the railway lines. It will be permanent. Eight thousand tiny LED lights will slowly ripple from red to green as trains pass by. One of the few obstacles remaining to the project is that the railway company still has to grant permission for the last installation. Robert Barnes explains proudly: 'They think it might be a safety hazard, distracting train drivers as they approach Paddington'.

Every designer has learnt to live with the fact
that ideas take time to mature. But after all that
thought and planning – when the idea is finally ready –
who wants to wait around another couple of years
for time to accomplish the desired effect?

The lively, light quality of a genuine copper patina
gives buildings a unique aesthetic charm.
The only problem being that it usually takes many
years of exposure to the air for the patina to develop.
For those with less patience, KME has done away
with the waiting times. TECU®- Patina are naturally
patinated copper products with all the positive qualities
of classical copper. For roofs, facades and interior design.

TECU®- Patina is pure natural green from the very beginning.
Now, only your ideas need time to mature.

ever in green

KME – Technical
Customer Service:
Tel. +49 541 321-43 23
Fax +49 541 321-40 30

KM Europa Metal AG
Postfach 33 20
D - 49023 Osnabrück

Internet
http: // www.kme.de

newMetropolis,
Amsterdam

Architect:
Renzo Piano

Product information:
KME UK Ltd.
9/17 Tuxford Road
Hamilton Industrial Park
GB - Leicester LE4 7TZ
Tel. +44 116 246 1130
Fax +44 116 246 1132
Telex 347077

TECU®- Classic
TECU®- Oxid
TECU®- Patina
TECU®- Zinn
TECU®- Shingles

TECU®
Creative coverage.

ARCHITECTURAL PRINCIPLES IN THE AGE OF HUMANISM

Rudolf Wittkower

Fourth edition

The new edition of this classic bestseller, the culmination of a lifetime of studies on Renaissance architecture by this gifted historian, is being published to coincide with the release of *Architectonics of Humanism*. Since its original publication the book has acquired the status of a classic, having brought to light, through exemplary scholarship, the connections between the architecture and the culture of the Renaissance. Professor Wittkower has produced definitive explanations of the true significance of certain architectural forms and at the same time revealed the limitations of a purely aesthetic theory of Renaissance architecture. Superbly reproduced in a large square format, this edition integrates for the first time the illustrations with the text.

'No other book on the subject of architectural history written by scholars of his generation has had such a creative effect on men in practice.' Nikolaus Pevsner, foreword to *Art and Architecture in Italy*.

'Professor Wittkower's mind is not only inquiring, but immensely well stored and tenacious. His studies of humanist architecture are masterpieces of scholarship.' Sir Kenneth Clark, *The Architectural Review*.

- New Edition of the classic bestseller
- Publication coincides with *Architectonics of Humanism*, Lionel March
- Stimulating text and images, with previously unpublished extracts from his lectures

PB 0471 97763 2, 242 x 224 mm, approx 160 pages. Illustrated throughout, mainly in colour. Y32.50 $32.50 £24.95: Autumn 1998

ARCHITECTONICS OF HUMANISM

Lionel March

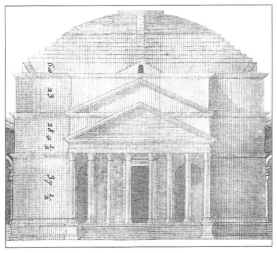

A vital reinterpretation of the architectural principles (the architectonics) of the Renaissance period, this book presents fresh views on the use of symmetry and proportion in the work of Alberti and Palladio, supported by new examples and illustrations. In the light of this new evaluation, the subsequent development of the Renaissance tradition into the 20th century moves away from Le Corbusier and the French school (Wittkower's position) towards its continuation and transformation in the Viennese and Chicago practices, exemplified by the work of Frank Lloyd Wright and the American school. The lively text is extensively illustrated and mathematical arguments are presented pictorially in the manner of many Renaissance texts.

- Significant new architectural theory
- Presented as a complementary, standard text on Renaissance architecture
- Stimulating text and images

PB 0471 97754 3, 242 x 224 mm, approx 160 pages. Illustrated throughout. Y45.00 $45.00 £24.95: Autumn 1998

CABLE NETS STRUCTURES

Maritz Vandenberg
DETAIL IN BUILDING

The fifth title in the *Detail in Building* series (which has previously focused on staircases, soft canopies, glass canopies, and columns) provides a historical overview and definition of cable net structures. The author, who was formerly Technical Editor of *The Architects' Journal*, explains in detail how to design the structures, how to evaluate costs per square metre, appropriate use of cable net structures and of their coverings. This is followed by eight intensive case studies which reflect the best design and use of cable net structures.

- An essential guide for architects and structural engineers
- Unusual and innovative case studies
- Part of the *Detail in Building* series

PB 0471 97823 X, 245 x 245 mm, 96 pages. Y32.50 $32.50 £18.99: Autumn 1998

THE EVERYDAY AND ARCHITECTURE

AD Profile 134
Guest-edited by Sarah Wigglesworth and Jeremy Till

In recent years, the everyday has become an important subject of social and philosophical theory. Eschewing the grand narratives and self-referential discourses which typify much theory, the everyday offers a productive area of research. This issue of *Architectural Design* investigates the habitual aspects of the built existence within which we live and work, revealing how everyday materials are often overlooked in favour of the extraordinary.
While this volume seeks to provide a theoretical grounding of the subject, it will nonetheless concentrate on the products of such thinking – these range from the popular, fun and eclectic aspects of the everyday to consideration of the impact of recycling on design as a serious question for society.

- Traces the historical development of the everyday in architecture
- Absorbing collection of essays and projects
- Fully illustrated survey

PB 0471 97708 X, 305 x 252 mm, 112 pages. $29.95 £18.99: July/August 1998

Exhibitions

RESPONSIVE ARCHITECTURE AT THE CROWBAR

THE BARTLETT SCHOOL OF ARCHITECTURE – UNIT 14

University College London

Unit 14 at The Bartlett continues a tradition of employing machine logic and machine intelligence to explore Cybernetic models of the built environment. Much of the work is concerned with the relationship between information and form, and in particular, dynamic form.

The gallery space at Exmouth Market is a single, rectangular room accessed both from the pedestrianised street market and from the coffee bar, and is marked by a long, narrow 'conference' table and a glass frontage. For the exhibition, the room was divided into a set of two- and three-dimensional 'sensory' zones in order to create an artificial environment with the capacity to respond to the various activities of its guests.

Events

From the coffee bar, the room was entered via an electronic 'whispering gallery', where feedback and delay were used to alter the acoustic properties of the space by 'throwing' the sounds received from a powerful uni-directional microphone to a remote-output location.

The room also had feelings. It was able to display one of three moods according to the number of occupants – its 'pulse-rate' could be felt as a vibration emitted at low frequency through a sub-woofer.

The room could also hear you by recording localised ambient noise from a mesh of miniature, omni-directional microphones whose digital codes were plotted as a 'colour cloud' inside a virtual representation of the room. The computation was done in real time and was displayed on a computer monitor.

The room could touch you, through the use of interactive coffee cups which were able to tell you whether or not you were entering a particular zone.

Its 'central nervous system' consisted of eight cells – mounted on the conference table – each of which could adopt any one of three possible states according to the number and location of visitors to the room.

Design

Each of the eight cells in this system was designed to function as an autonomous entity, but at the same time programmed to respond to both environmental inputs (when approached or touched it responded) and electronic data (it responded to digital signals from its neighbours). This enabled the whole group of cells to produce responsive behaviour of a type that was unpredictable since collective behaviour then 'emerged' from the relationship of the individuals to each other and to the outside world.

'Cellular activity' was represented by the motions of elastic rods driven simultaneously in air and water by a servo-motor. In air, each rod could detect tiny fluctuations in light levels and avoid shading its neighbour in much the same way as would a leaf or a tree. Underwater, the activity was harnessed to influence the movement of synthetic, cellular forms that were designed to behave like a secondary liquid.

At any time, the 'mood' of any cell was reflected in a simple facial gesture that was viewed through a semi-reflective, glass screen.

Computation

The computer program that controls the cells is a 'state machine' that works by first expressing a state and then observing the effects of that expression, before deciding whether to remain in that state or to react to its observations by changing state.

The software for the state-machine determines what the cells should do with their observations in the form of a rule-base. Visitors are the principal environmental stimuli, detected through an array of floor pressure pads that become the input to each cell's rule-base.

For example, if a cell is in its bored state and there is floor input local to it, then it will jump to a state of being content. If the floor input stays at that level, it will remain in the content state. If the floor input increases, it will jump to being in an excited state where it will remain until the floor input decreases.

The software also controls the collection of the observations which feed the rule-base and consequently drives the behaviour of each cell. A real-time response was possible by interlacing observations about itself and its environment with its reaction to them.

Pete Silver, Chris Leung, Andrew Whiting

The work was exhibited during Architecture Week (21-27 November, 1997) at Crowbar Coffee, Exmouth Market

Exhibitions

MAPS + MOVIES AT GRAND CENTRAL TERMINAL

NEW YORK CITY

Louise Braverman Architects

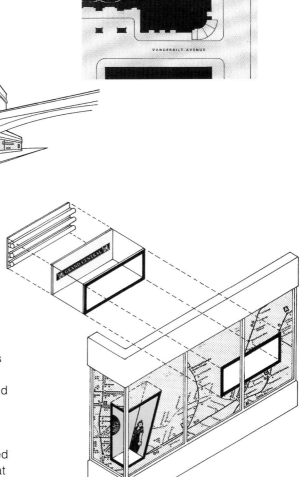

This installation, which received the 'Best Category for Environments Award' for the 1997 ID Design Review Awards, explores the interface of function and fantasy at Grand Central Terminal through its display of interwoven layers of information.

Braverman's previous installation, entitled *Poetic Light*, had been located adjacent to the main concourse of the terminal the year before. This project consisted of a 45-foot-long glass enclosure with multicoloured planes of light, through which moved a continuous loop of poetic verse on a coloured background. The installation's objective was to address the inherent contradiction of encountering poetry.

Maps + Movies juxtaposes utilitarian railroad transit maps with cinematic stills filmed at the terminal, communicating the diverse ways in which Grand Central Terminal itself affects the lives of New York City pedestrians.

The site for the installation is the area behind six glass storefronts on the 42nd Street facade of the terminal. Its length is about 300 feet and its depth roughly four feet. While creating a screening device to mask the construction work in progress for the next several years behind the storefronts, the installation engages the passerby with two strata of information

and aesthetics about Grand Central Terminal.

In effect, the windows become a light beacon, drawing the commuter towards the glass. Up close, the pedestrian sees two layers of information. The glass surface of the storefronts are back-lighted and covered with translucent mylar, recurrently screened with an image of a railroad transit map. Three-dimensional recessed translucent panels, silkscreened with images from motion pictures filmed at the terminal, intermittently pierce the translucent mylar, creating 'windows' into its cultural heritage.

Reviews

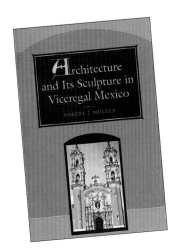

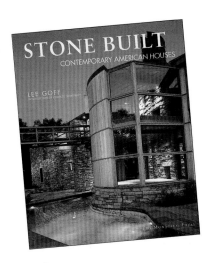

Architecture and its Sculpture in Viceregal Mexico, *Robert J Mullen, University of Texas Press (Texas), 286pp, b/w ills, HB $45.00, PB $24.95*

This volume provides an overview of the churches and civic buildings of the colonial period in Mexico (1535-1821), concentrating primarily on the history, spatial organisation and distinctive features of the churches and cathedrals, which are described by the author in graphic detail. These buildings can be seen to reflect the freedom of religious orders in this part of the world as parishes began to replace missions, and friars were responsible to their superior rather than under the control of the bishop.

It is estimated that around 10 million people had been converted to the Catholic faith within 50 years of the arrival of the Spanish friars. Mullen relates that as a result of the mass conversions 'on some days the friar's arm had to be propped up in order for him to continue pouring the baptismal waters'. He explains that in certain cases, imaginary walls served to define the church, with the altar contained within a roofed structure and the 'west wall' marked by a raised cross.

A frenzy of building activity ensued in response to the desperate need for church buildings. Although construction methods of the church proper at this time (mostly single nave, rectangular structures) were relatively simple, a considerable number of open-air churches were erected to serve a temporary role. Mullen's selection of these is extensive, ranging from large-scale constructions such as the huge San José de los Naturales in Mexico City – which was able to accommodate the catafalque for Charles V's funeral services – to the little Capilla de Indios in Tlaxcala: a building with two choirs, distinguished by the Franciscan use of the ogee arch, a particularly Moorish feature. Mullen observes that these open-air churches were highly effective in the transition to the catholic faith of a culture accustomed to ceremonies outside. Examples of this building type, which is unique to Mexico, continued to be used to accommodate worshippers on feast days.

The content of the book is stimulating, communicating the way in which European cultural techniques were commonly fused with indigenous pre-Hispanic elements and symbols, especially in the pueblos' churches. Not surprisingly, in the wake of a somewhat rapid conversion, the architecture was shaped with various degrees of sophistication. Whilst the book succeeds in addressing this eclectic architectural mix (which was able to appeal to both cultures with its hybrid iconography) at no stage does the reader gain a sense of the adverse effects of colonial intervention, which the author may have deemed irrelevant to his focus.

The subject matter is organised into six main chapters. The reader is introduced to the urban beginnings and the formative era (16th century): a time when buildings such as hospitals were remarkable for their social rather than architectural organisation. The focus then shifts to the architecture and sculpture of the cathedrals: 'symbols of authority' ranging from the austere to the heavily embellished. The transitional phase is then examined (mid-17th to mid-18th century), distinguished by such luscious grotto-like creations as the Capilla del Rosario in the church of Santo Domingo in Puebla (1690), where the art of relief in stucco was developed to perfection. The last two chapters explore The Age of Fulfilment, 1730-1800, touching briefly on the 'silver' churches and the monumental residences and haciendas; and finally, frontier mission architecture, revealing the impact of native building on Spanish colonial architecture, especially in the pueblo world around Santa Fe.

Although the book is very readable, its content is structured more in the manner of a travel guide or reference volume, with individual buildings neatly categorised. The publication is peppered throughout with black and white photographs but their quality varies considerably; indeed, many of the pictures fail to do justice to the clarity of Mullen's text. Inspirational subject matter of this kind would clearly benefit from the use of colour illustrations. However, this would inevitably raise the price of a book that is unpretentious and, in its present form, affordable for students.

Iona Spens

Reversible Destiny – Arakawa / Gins, *Introductions by Michael Govan and Jean-François Lyotard, Guggenheim Museum Publications (New York), 1997, 324pp, colour ills*

The work of the poet and philosopher Madeline Gins and artist Shusaku Arakawa challenges the fundamental nature of our relationship with the world around us. Having moved into the field of architecture, collaborative efforts such as the outdoor park in Japan, *Site of Reversible Destiny–Yoro* (1993-95), succeed,

Reviews
Books

quite literally, in throwing us off balance.

Arakawa and Gins propose that the primary purpose of life in our time should be 'to not to die', and that we must 'learn how not to die' by reversing the course of conventional destiny. The scope of this book is extensive, offering a compelling and provocative insight into the domain of the 'architectural body' (defined as the body proper plus the architectural surround). In addition to the diverse range of projects and texts by Arakawa and Gins, this generously illustrated volume includes essays by Andrew Benjamin, George Lakoff, Greg Lynn and Jesse Reiser among others.

Stone Built: Contemporary American Houses,
Lee Goff, The Monacelli Press (New York), 1997, 272pp, colour ills, £40
This title highlights the use of stone in contemporary American residences, with examples of 27 exteriors and interiors. These are distributed into four sections: urban/suburban, country, water, and mountains.

As a result of the introduction of steel in the mid-19th century and the need for insulation, stone tended to be used as a cladding material rather than for structural purposes. A fraction of the houses illustrated in this volume have solid stone walls, nevertheless, they succeed in conveying the enduring quality of the material.

The bulk of the book comprises a visual exploration, making the most of a stunning collection of photographs. This is preceded by a brief history of stone houses in the USA and a short introduction by the architect Charles Gwathmey.

Designing for the Disabled: The New Paradigm,
Selwyn Goldsmith, Butterworth Heinemann (Oxford), 1997, 426pp, b/w ills, HB £45.00
In the wake of Goldsmith's previous study *Designing for the Disabled*, published in 1963, the UK Government introduced for-the-disabled accessibility legislation. This, Goldsmith demonstrates, has proven to be technically faulty and socially discriminatory.

In this edition the author sets out to resolve the situation and suggests that the Government should discard its current regulatory controls and put in place comprehensive new regulations which would ensure that buildings are convenient for all users.

Goldsmith compares the situation with that in the USA, highlighting the problems encountered by Britain in attempting to follow a similar path.

Although the thrust of the book relates to public buildings – most aspects of which seems to have been covered in this somewhat dense volume – the concept of accessible housing is also addressed, as are alterations to existing buildings. The objective of this study is to encourage architects to discard the conventional methods that have been applied to this area of design.

Robert A M Stern: Houses,
Robert A M Stern, The Monacelli Press (New York), 1998, 608pp, HB £50
This weighty volume features over 30 of Robert Stern's houses from the 1970s to the present day. Stern is an architect who abhors the 'false modernism' that exists, believing that 'buildings give meaning to the present by connecting to the past'. In a brief and personal introduction, he emphasises the importance of houses and in particular the context. This is followed by a series of projects which are presented with a portfolio of stimulating colour photographs that leave nothing to the imagination. Each project is accompanied by a short but lively description written by the architect.

The book is really a visual feast of Stern's work, and should be appreciated as such. The selection of residences is diverse but reveals a sense of architectural continuity, bearing the imprint of an architect with one foot in the past who seeks to reinterpret it anew.

Back to Earth, Adobe Building in Saudi Arabia,
William Facey, with an introduction by Prince Sultan bin Salman bin 'Abd al-'Aziz Al Sa'ud, IB Tauris & Co (London)1998, 216pp, HB £50
This book addresses the role of the vernacular style in modern architecture, relating in detail a restoration programme that was undertaken at a neglected old farmhouse at al-'Udhaibat. It outlines the attempt to create an adobe house adapted to the needs of modern living while able to exploit the advantages of modern technology.

Once owned by the late King Faisal, the project for this modest farmhouse is viewed as a test-bed for the application of the adoble building method today, its performance under constant scrutiny. Traditional techniques of adobe building are examined in the book alongside close examination of the rebuilding process. While presented as a useful case study, this restoration scheme acts as a springboard for an indigenous architecture of the future.

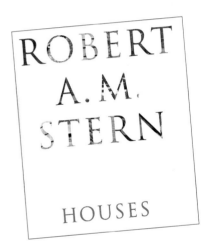

Reviews
Books

Arts and Crafts Gardens, *Wendy Hitchmough, Pavilion Books Limited (London), 1997, 208pp, colour ills, HB £30*

Today, gardens tend to be synonymous with 'lifestyle' or leisure rather than architectural design or even gardening itself. There is a wider public for the media and garden-related activities than horticulture or a real love and knowledge of plants. Magazine-style TV programmes, 'living' sections of Sunday broadsheets, sumptuous garden centres, upmarket holidays and the most prestigious trade fair, the Chelsea Flower Show, all feed the armchair gardener's unrequitable consumer desires. Aren't we all seduced and tantalised by images of the wealthy's garden paradises featured in interior design and garden magazines?

The demise of the country house and the importation of a European notion of exterior space – a balcony or roof terrace – has placed the garden largely outside the more progressive architect's urban sphere and made it an unfashionable and bourgeois consideration. The most notable exception to this in recent years has been Charles Jencks' 'garden of cosmic speculation' on the Scottish Borders. However, this is largely an intellectual venture, as the garden explores landscape metaphors for scientific theory. It is concerned with the academic rather than the spatial aspect of architecture in a horticultural context.

What Wendy Hitchmough does in *Arts and Crafts Gardens* is rediscover a view of the garden, taken up at the end of the last century by architects and garden designers, capable of simultaneously embracing the philosophical and the spatial. Central to her approach is her notion of the Arts and Crafts Movement's formulation of the garden as 'an outdoor room'.

This concept is most aptly and lyrically described by Hitchmough herself:

> The principle of a house connected to the landscape, where the lines and materials of the building spread like surface roots into the walls and pathways of the garden, and where the sharp divisions between interior and exterior space were exploded in open-air living rooms that projected like decks over the landscape.

This, combined with a revival of interest in natural planting, which was partly a response to the Victorians' obsession with exotic specimens, was the most predominant characteristic of the Arts and Crafts garden.

Though Hitchmough is quite clear in her definition of an 'Arts and Crafts garden', she asserts a bold and broad conception of the actual movement. Rather than sticking to the style-bound period, traditionally received by art historians to be the two decades at the turn of the century, she traces its origins to William Morris' and Philip Webb's Red House in the 1850s. This shows that the Arts and Crafts garden was not conceived in a vacuum, and portrays it as a dynamic, forever-changing medium. Her account takes in the fashion for the old-fashioned among the aesthetic movement of the 1860s, the new interest in natural planting awakened by William Robinson after 1870 and the move towards the architectural treatment of gardens, before in Gertrude Jekyll's work, 'gardening was elevated to an art and became an integral part of the Arts and Crafts Movement'.

In her preface, the author states that hers is not an encyclopaedic treatment of the subject. It is not her intention to include all gardens that could be termed Arts and Crafts within the one volume. An architectural historian, who has written a major work on CFA Voysey and detailed studies of the Michelin and Hoover Buildings, Hitchmough is more intent on exploring the progressive cultural contexts of the gardens themselves. This makes far more interesting reading – Hitchmough has a gift for writing accessibly on an academic subject – she not only looks at the ideas that shaped the planning of the gardens but also their social environment. She points out that ironically many of the country houses, which pursued a return to nature and the vernacular in their building methods and style, were built with money from industry and commerce. A recurring theme throughout is the opportunities that the Arts and Crafts garden offered women, personified by possibly the most important figure in the movement, Gertrude Jekyll.

Perhaps one of the strongest aspects of this book is Hitchmough's discussion of the gardens themselves. For the most pivotal designs (Red House, Gravetye Manor, Hidcote . . .) descriptions are supplied that amount to the reader being accompanied around the gardens with the author. With her own words, Hitchmough enables us to experience the gardens as she herself has done. She is unhindered by her research or any temptation to blind us with Latin labels in conveying extant layouts and planting. Her concern for clarification and immediacy is further supported by carefully drawn plans and photographs.

Martin Charles' photographs alone are reason enough to purchase this title. Capturing both entire views and details, they are presented to create a beautiful visual record of the subject. What, however, is rare and invaluable is the degree to which the author and photographer have collaborated. The photographs not only illustrate the gardens but particular aspects of them described in the text. For instance, the density of 'wild' planting at Gravetye is shown in a photograph and there is a picture of the south-facing wall at Hestercombe which creates a vertical border with lavender, catmint, erigeron and santolina.

Above all, it is the impressive assimilation of the book's various elements that contributes to its success. It is apparent that in every aspect, the title has been conceived with the reader in mind. At the back, there is a list of all of the houses and gardens included with not only the dates and architects names but their opening times and telephone numbers. With a format that is slightly smaller and squarer than A4, it is a coffee table book that begs a read and can still be easily handled.

Helen Castle

HYPERSURFACE ARCHITECTURE

STUDIO ASYMPTOTE, WRITING SPACE: INSTALLATION, PAPER BIENNALE, DÜREN, GERMANY

Architectural Design

HYPERSURFACE ARCHITECTURE

OPPOSITE: MARCOS NOVAK, WARP MAP
ABOVE: KAS OOSTERHUIS, SALT WATER PAVILION, NEELTJE JANS, THE NETHERLANDS

ACADEMY EDITIONS • LONDON

Acknowledgements

We would like to express our gratitude to all the contributors to *Architectural Design*, and in particular Stephen Perrella for guest-editing this issue.

Photographic Credits: Microsoft/Softimage kindly allowed their Softimage animation software to be used. Unless otherwise stated all material is courtesy of the authors and architects. Attempts have been made to locate the sources of all photographs to obtain full reproduction rights, but in the very few cases where this process has failed to find the copyright holder, our apologies are offered. Paul Cumming *p11 below*; Venturi, Scott Brown and Associates, Inc, Anderson/Schwartz Architects, TAMS Consultants, Inc *p11 above*; Tomio Ohashi *p13 above*; Dimitri Aronov, Jeffrey Cook, Sam de Silva, Ross Johnson, Narinder Singh, Roam Cam (SVHS), Wendy Spencer, Gary Zebington *p13 centre*; Didier Boy de la Tour *p13 below*; Marc Treib/Fondation Le Corbusier *p17 below*; Eeva-Liisa Pelkonen/Fondation Jean Dubuffet *p21 above, centre (1)*; Ezra Stoller/Museum of Modern Art, New York *p21 centre (2), below*; City of New York *p29 centre*; Scott Frances/Esto *p36 below*; Cees van Gliessen *p71*; Pierre Berenger *p74 above, p75 below*; Gilles Ehrmann *p76 below*; Gerald Zugman *p94*; Tom Wiscombe *p95*

I am grateful for the encouragement of Bernard Tschumi and Columbia University GSAP, and the efforts and assistance of Rebecca Carpenter, Paul Cumming, Dennis Pang and Kunio Kudo, and the support of David Buege, the V2_Organisation, Melissa McMahon and the Australasian Society for Continental Philosophy. For their research feedback and colleagueship, I would like to thank Marcos Novak, Lars Spuybroek, Joke Brouwer, John Beckmann, Gary Genosko, Brian Massumi, Michael Speaks, Andrew Benjamin, Greg Ulmer, Bernard Cache, Frederic Migayrou, Ron Evitts, Odile Fillion, Laetitia Wolff, Chloé Parent, Terence Riley, John Lobell, Arakawa and Madeline Gins, Tom Klinkowstein, Igor Cronsoie, Steve Calvanico, Ciro Asperti, Robert Corbett, Katherine Demetriou, Katrin Kalden and my business partner Paul Lieberman. I am very grateful to Dr Alan Bass for showing me the difference between an intellectual view of Otherness and one that can be embraced within life. I would also like to acknowledge the support and interest of Bruce Giltin, President of Milgo-Bufkin metalworks, who in conjunction with Baldev Duggal, President of Duggal Photo, Inc and Hannah Schlusser, are currently helping to build the first hypersurface prototypes.   *Stephen Perrella*

Front Cover: Stephen Perrella, The Möbius House Study
Back Cover: Kas Oosterhuis, Salt Water Pavilion, Neeltje Jans, The Netherlands
Inside Covers: Nox Architects, FreshH$_2$O eXPO (Fresh Water Pavilion), Zeeland,
The Netherlands

EDITOR: Maggie Toy
DEPUTY EDITOR: Ellie Duffy
DESIGN: Mario Bettella and Andrea Bettella/Artmedia

First published in Great Britain in 1998 by *Architectural Design*
42 LEINSTER GARDENS, LONDON W2 3AN

A division of John Wiley & Sons
Baffins Lane, Chichester, West Sussex PO19 1UD

ISBN: 0-471-97809-4

The Publishers and Editor do not hold themselves responsible for the opinions expressed by
the writers of articles or letters in this magazine
Copyright of articles and illustrations may belong to individual writers or artists
Architectural Design Profile 133 is published as part of
Architectural Design Vol 68 5-6 /1998
Architectural Design Magazine is published six times a year and is available by subscription

Printed and bound in Italy

Contents

ARCHITECTURAL DESIGN PROFILE No 133
HYPERSURFACE ARCHITECTURE
Guest-edited by Stephen Perrella

Stephen Perrella, Studio AEM, The Institute for Electronic Clothing, 1990 (with Anthony Wong and Ed Keller)

STEPHEN PERRELLA
HYPERSURFACE THEORY: ARCHITECTURE><CULTURE

*Nike's marketing strategy develops both form (product develop-
ment), follows market and the reverse – first the creation of image
and lifestyles (creating the market) and then the design of the
products that support that lifestyle change. For example, a kid in
Harlem plays basketball, Nike re-presents that image, markets it
and that image comes back to the court, and now the kid is
wearing Nike shoes.* John Hoke, Nike Marketing Strategist[1]

*In curved space, the shortest distance between two points is a
curved line.* Albert Einstein

E-mail (excerpt) to Brian Massumi, September 1997
In architecture, there has been a tendency to eschew
vulgar capitalist programmes: that is, to avoid the contamination of everyday consumer praxis, to stand-off from it, and
somehow establish higher cultural ground. This, of course,
describes a specific course through the last 60 years of modernism
but is generally a basic aspiration. Over the last 10 years or so,
with the advent of Derridean and post-structuralist thought,
architecture, through a discourse established by only a small
group of critics, has exacted a questioning of architecture's
logocentrism leading to the movement known as 'Deconstructionist
architecture'. Although the effect was pervasive in academia, a
few of the architectural theoreticians were unsatisfied, believing
that architecture still possessed a material presence that was not
accommodated by the language/textually oriented philosophy of
Derrida. They therefore moved towards the thinking of Gilles
Deleuze and Félix Guattari, to improvise a radical theory that
addressed architecture in its materiality. My sense all along has
been that these improvisations are too narrow a reading of
Deleuze, reflected in the theories of Greg Lynn and Peter
Eisenman. However, as Deleuze's concept of The Fold became
the main focus of theoretical architecture and computer technology
became pervasive, we began to see in architecture, a clear move
into topology. Many of the designs produced (especially here at
Columbia GSAP) assumed smoother and more landscaped forms.

My concern with this was that it still continued an Enlightenment
modernist tendency to avoid the messiness and vulgarity of
everyday consumer praxis, an issue that Robert Venturi and
Denise Scott Brown tried to bring into the consciousness of
architecture. And so, the saturation of the Internet and the
spread of teletechnology into regular business practices were
not quite able to find their way into these topological, architectural design processes. However, as a journalist-architect, I am
more inclined to embrace the radical proliferation of everyday
advertisements or sign-culture as they connect to ever greater
interfaces, or what we now witness as the emergence of a media
culture. I also wondered how architecture's reading of Deleuze
could possibly accommodate these semiotic mutations from
everyday praxis, inasmuch as Deleuzean thought is concerned
with opening boundaries and unfolding surfaces into conditions

of pure exteriority. Having a Heideggerian/Derridian background,
I interpreted the media proliferation as an auto-deconstruction;
that is, the deconstruction of the capitalist subject through the
very modes of production and technologies that proliferate due
to the instrumentalism inherent in consumer economics. Therefore, it seems the action at the level of the street, a hitherto
neutralised element of the architectural problem, is becoming a
contaminating factor, and the problem is that architecture,
because of its formalist tradition, does not know how to respond
to or embrace the technologically deconstructed or deterritorialised
consumer subject. Yet arguably, these 'media' forces are pres-
surising the sanctity of elite architecture (and of course every
other discipline) to enter into formative processes. This is why I
am attempting to conjoin these two trajectories – mediatised
culture and topological architecture – into an intertwined
dynamic, one that I have come to call hypersurface. Your writings
in *Capitalism and Schizophrenia: A User's Guide*, and Gary
Genosko's readings of Félix Guattari, convinced me that there
was, in fact, a semiotic and experiential dimension to Deleuze
and Guattari that was missing from the initial and perhaps biased
reading by architectural theorists, which resulted in a privileging
of unadorned topology. While I truly support the topological
impulses, I also realise that unless architecture is connected to
everyday life, it is not alive, or even animate. For this reason I
seek your consideration, and Gary's, to assist me with this
second reading, so that architecture does not miss all the rich
effects of a radical empiricism, as it concerns new forms of
experience.

Hypersurface: architecture><culture
Hypersurface is an emerging architectural/cultural condition that
is effected through an intertwining of often opposing realms of
language and matter into irresolvable complexities that create
middle-out conditions. In an effort to avoid thematising this effect
and to consider it in its fullest complexity, the term hypersurface
is introduced, to describe and render productive an Otherness
that resists classical definitions but that is simultaneously produced by the tenets of traditional culture. As a verb, hypersurface
considers ways in which the realm of representation (read
images) and the realm of instrumentality (read forms) are respectively becoming deconstructed and deterritorialised into new
image-forms of intensity. Hypersurfaces are an interweaving and
subsequent unlocking of culturally-instituted dualities.
Hypersurface theory is not a subjective invention, in contrast to
what seems an unending foray of 'isms' attempting to explain
postmodern culture (for instance in the efforts of Charles Jencks).
Instead, this research suggests that there are self-generating
and auto-emergent forces deeply insinuated within cultural
historicity that are being unleashed by the machinations of
contemporary praxis, and which already present a formidable
challenge to the authority of the designer. Binary relations in

Western culture, as in the relationships between image and form, trace a long tradition leading to schizophrenic dichotomisation. Hypersurface theory may work productively with the effects and mutations that occur as a result of an accelerating capitalism. Hypersurfaces are configured, immanative topologies constituting nondialectic image-form interfaces into which intersubjectivity is being absorbed, only to re-emerge autopoeitically.

Hypersurface is a reconsideration of often dichotomous relationships existing in the environment. These binaries include: image/form, inside/outside, structure/ornament, ground/edifice and so forth; not as separate and hence static entities but as transversally-constituted fabrics or planes of immanence. Hypersurfaces are generated in the problematic relationships that occur when binary categories conjugate because such divisions can no longer be sustained in isolation through either linguistic or material divisions. Categories of the Real and the Unreal, for instance, are insufficient today because each is infused within the other. The reality of a Disney phantasm superposed with the unreality of media constructs, such as the O J Simpson incident, begin to describe a process of debasement brought about by deeply-rooted cultural contradictions – indeed, a schizophrenia.

The mechanisms that drive the real through the unreal and vice versa, impairing both, stem from the accelerating force of ubiquitous, everyday consumer-culture. This is what leads such theorists as Frederic Jameson and Mark Wigley to describe our contemporary condition as one of being 'lost in space'. A more accurate description, however, would be that we are 'lost at home', because there are no longer clear insides or outsides, and it is from the contortions within this context that immanent forces now issue forth. Such events are described here as hypersurfaces, producing intensities that are tangible, vital, phenomenological (or proprioceptive) experiences of space-time-information.

AntiTRANSCENDENTal defections
In mathematics, a hypersurface is a surface in hyperspace, but in the context of this journal the mathematical term is existentialised. Hyperspace is four + dimensional space, but here hypersurfaces are rethought to render a more complex notion of space-time-information. This reprogramming is motivated by cultural forces that have the effect of superposing existential sensibilities onto mathematical and material conditions, especially the recent topological explorations of architectural form. The proper mathematical meaning of the term hypersurface is discussed here as being challenged by an inherently subversive dynamic within capitalism. While in mathematics, hypersurfaces exist in 'higher', or hyperdimensions, the abstractness of these mathematical dimensions is shifting, defecting or devolving into our lived cultural context. Situated in this newly prepared context, hypersurface comes to define a new condition of human agency, of post-humanism: one that results from the internal machinations of consumer culture, thereby transforming prior conditions of an assumed stability. Instead of meaning higher in an abstract sense, 'Hyper' means altered. In both contexts, ideal abstraction and the life-world, operation is in relation to normal three-space (x, y, z). In mathematics there are direct, logical progressions from higher to lower dimensions. In an existential context, hyper might be understood as arising from a lived-world conflict as it mutates the normative dimensions of three-space, into the dominant construct that organises culture. In abstract mathspace we

have 'dimensional' constructs, in cultural terms we have 'existential' configurations; but the dominance of the mathematical model is becoming contaminated because the abstract realm can no longer be maintained in isolation. The defection of the meaning of hypersurface, as it shifts to a more cultural/existential sense, entails a reworking of mathematics. (This is similar to what motivates Deleuze to reread Leibniz.) This defection is a deconstruction of a symbolic realm into a lived one; not through any casual means: it arises and is symptomatic of the failure of our operative systemics to negotiate the demands placed upon it. If one could describe an event whereby cultural activities could act upon abstractions so as to commute the normative, etymological context into a context of lived dynamics, what activity has that capability? The term hypersurface is not simply attributed new meaning, but instead results from a catastrophic defection from a realm of linguistic ideality (mathematics). If ideals, as they are held in a linguistic realm, can no longer support or sustain their purity and disassociation, then such terms and meanings begin, in effect, to 'fall from the sky'. This is to describe the deterritorialisation of idealisation into a more material real. In the new sense for hypersurface, 'hyper' is not in binary relation to surface, it is a new reading that describes a complex condition within architectural surfaces in our contemporary life-world.

Capitalism and schizophrenia
The cultural forces leading to conditions that now evoke hypersurfaces are complex but may be traced through one main bifurcation in particular, one among many, that is formative in the history of Western culture. The division is between architecture as a formal practice and the practices of everyday life. Theorist-historians Alberto Perez-Gomez, Christian Norberg-Schulz and Robin Evans offer some of the most compelling accounts of the constellation of issues that this bifurcation involves. The overt result is that architecture comes to sustain an idea about form based upon its own internal discourse, one increasingly disassociated with the meaning structures constituted in the everyday world of commerce and material practices.

Our current architectural values tend to continue the division between the (capitalist) programme on the one hand, and (elite) form-making on the other. There have been many attempts to overcome this division within modern architecture. Strategies such as the 'form follows function' dictum stemming from Mies van der Rohe, while affirming everyday activities, remain complicit with the assumptions of capitalist progressivism prior to any interpretation of function or programme (one merely accepts the capitalist programme and expresses it). The modernist tactic privileges one oppositional term over another (driven by the obvious instrumentalism in the term 'follow') and is how binary thought works in the service of transcendentality. (In typical dialectics the synthesis of binary oppositions aspires to ascend to an ideal, one attended to by an ideality, like God.) But any process that assumes an ideality as an ultimate end is doomed to failure, inasmuch as it is ultimately unattainable. Yet this has remained the mandate of Western thought and has pervaded every value structure. Thus schizophrenia, sustained by capitalism, is continually forwarded by any attempt to synthesise a resolution with which to heal the fundamental split between form and programme. One of the least-considered strategies with which to negotiate perpetual dichotomisation (as it is reinscribed in the built environment) is to accept the schizophrenic condition, instead of attempting incessantly to overcome or transcend it with further, rational methodologies.

Dichotomisation can easily be read in the architectural cladding of Western culture. If we consider what architecture has historically symbolised – that is, what its form/surface relation has signified – it could be argued that form-surfaces (a prioritisation of structure over skin) have been at the service of the institutional power or a metaphysical belief behind a particular architectural institution. Architectural surfaces (of a religious, public or private institution) are thoroughly coordinated representations whether they are structurally expressive as in the case of Gothic architecture, or metaphorical as in the case of recent postmodern styles. Again, what seems most characteristic of modernism, in many of it manifestations, is that its system of representation is one of instrumentality; form-follows-function structures signification to be subsumed within the form. This is precisely how the realm of signification or signs are interpreted for the sake of form (where geometry becomes a scaffold for a transcendental belief structure). But signs have another meaning and another context; one that is normally superposed over construction. The vulgar programme of architecture simultaneously sustains a signification system, better described by Jean Baudrillard and Umberto Eco. And so, this doubled systemic of structure and sign commingle, leaving us to construct identities within schizophrenic contingency.

In an attempt to supersede the hierarchy of structure over surface, architect Bernard Tschumi used structural glass in his Gröninger Museum video gallery, employing tactics of reversal and dynamisation. Inside, the video columns displace the traditional meaning of a column as body, into flickering signifiers adrift upon the gallery's night surface. This project is seminal in a move toward hypersurfaces: in particular, through the way in which it reconfigures traditional architectural assumptions. In Tschumi's work, form is negated in order to celebrate programme in a tactic of negative modernism that affirms the deterritorialised consumer-subject as an ornamented membrane. Tschumi's deconstruction of traditional hierarchies in architecture reveals the latent potentialities of consumer praxis into an event space. His sensibility remains distinct, however, from the topological strategies of form that might carry his deconstructed and disseminated signifiers into contiguous surfaces. This possibility is taken up by other practices, notably in the work of Toyo Ito and Studio Asymptote, as well as Coop Himmelb(l)au. These are examples of architecture reaching towards consumer culture, remaining distinct from everyday consumer praxis reaching into architecture (unmediated by a designer). This is a propensity that architects may strive to engage, but in so doing may need to relinquish further degrees of authorship, as in the work and strategies of Bernard Cache, whose work raises the issue of the obsolescence of the architect altogether.

What appears to be a spreading trajectory is the further decentralisation of commercial representational systems unleashing new forms of human agency, in the guise of interactive information-play within the material surfaces of architecture. Nowhere is the possibility for such a transformative liberation (radical democratisation) so blatantly evident as in the electronic displays of New York's Times Square and Las Vegas (in particular the Freemont Street arcade). These are sites that Robert Venturi and Denise Scott Brown, Rem Koolhaas and philosopher Mark Taylor and numerous others have already investigated with varying degrees of architectural and philosophical import. (And it seem that the original impulse of Venturi/Scott Brown and

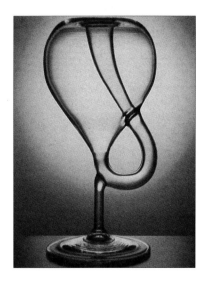

FROM ABOVE: XS cyber-arcade, Times Square – the schizophrenic condition between the real and the virtual; Steven Lisberger, Disney's Tron, 1982 – landscape with imbedded lines of information; Klein Bottle – topological space

Izenour – that is, to embrace the authenticity of vulgar culture – was quite prescient. Venturi's recent attempts, in his book *Iconographics and Electronics Upon a Generic Architecture*, to once more make architecture relevant to those who use it, was a move to embrace the dominant modes of signification for architecture. It was a move to democratise the discourse of architecture as walls to be written upon by those who inhabit it.) But while each, respectively, notes an underlying impetus within these deterritorialising contexts, their descriptions continue to embrace the extreme manifestations of capitalist culture as authentic and exhilarating (as almost all right or delirious). Yet we may ask what is offered in their descriptions to adequately negotiate a more deeply ingrained schizophrenia? The question is, to what extent do architects, who in an attempt to absorb 'vulgar' culture into the elite realm of architecture, only further subjugate capitalism's uncanny vitality into the formalisms of architectural discourse?

Hypersurface theory argues for planes of immanence (not planes of reference) whereby a vital relation between form and programme is a play of intensities (becomings) that are not commodifiable. Whether we are learning from (VSBA), delirious of (Koolhaas), or hidden because of (Taylor) the excesses of capitalism, the phenomenon and radicalisation of consumption in relation to the graphic sign (whether print, electric or electronic) can be seen as an activity that takes on self-transformative power; much in the manner of the Nike marketing strategy in the opening quote, but further accelerated. It is transformative in the way that older systems of representation used to work for institutions and the way that hyperconsumptive semiotics can serve to refigure an intersubjective self-image in an endless process of reconfiguration – indeed, disfiguration.

Incommensurates: architecture/culture
Hypersurface is an effect that occurs within the interface between two hitherto disparate trajectories of culture: in this case, the division between the aesthetic culture and academic discourse of architecture as distinct from the operations and machinations of everyday consumer culture. This is not an improvised separation, nor is it a forced dichotomy for argument's sake. Moreover, it is an attempt to identify and characterise the intertwining of two entirely different systems of subversion – one, avant-garde; the other, ordinary culture – taking place in two entirely different realms of culture but interfacing on the surface of built architecture. 'Hyper' implies human agency reconfigured by digital culture, and 'surface' is the enfolding of substances into differentiated topologies. The term hypersurface is not a concept that contains meaning, but is an event; one with a material dimension. We are currently at the threshold of this new configuration as a site of emergence for new intensities of culture and intersubjectivity. Toto Ito has recently written:

> Through the penetration of various new forms of media, fluidity is once again gaining validity. As more urban and architectural space is controlled by the media, it is becoming increasingly cinematic and fluid [. . .] On the one hand our material bodies are a primitive mechanism, taking in air and water and circulating them. On the other hand there is another kind of body which consists of circulating electronic information – the body that is connected to the rest of the world through various forms of media including microchips. Today we are being forced to think about how to architecturally combine these two different bodies and find an appropriate space for the emerging third body.

The third body that Ito describes is what is meant here by hypersurface. However, the body does not remain an operative metaphor going beyond what Deleuze and Guattari have called a 'body without organs'.

On the side of materiality, form has been pushed out of relation to function, programme has been dissuaded from context, and structure is disjoint from signification in any given architectural nexus. (This is clearly the impetus for the project presented here by Jesse Reiser and Nanako Umemoto – a seminal project that depicts more accurately the schizo-genesis that architectural problems seem now to require.) Architecture may now be explored as a condition of variant (human) agencies playing through, about and within one another; singular, yet connected and in a state of flux.

Provisionally, this may be called a condition of hypersurface. This trope serves only to accrue, absorb and resonate meaning, acting as an infrastructural term, a gesture toward a new middle ground between the traditionally conceived body/object duality. 'Hyper' suggests an existential eventualisation of the consumer-subject and 'surface' entails the new conditions of an object-in-relation. This is another way to consider Bernard Cache's theorisation of Subjectiles and Objectiles but with an added layer of complexity, in the incommensurate condition in which the two dynamised polarities commingle. Grafted, conjoined and co-determining the existent (the ecstatic subject) and the object-in-relation or hypersurface (dis)resonate together in a highly problematic, inflected condition.

Two main impulses operate simultaneously and contribute to the dynamic of hypersurfaces in architecture/culture. These two streams are reflected in elite architecture, predictably mapping the schizophrenia from the larger cultural context. The weaker trajectory (weaker because it goes against the dominant values of architecture as materiality, and the modernist subsumption of the sign within form) within the discipline of architecture is what has been elsewhere called 'pixel' architecture, that has been an attempt to manifest information space. In the current collection of projects, this trajectory is presented in the work of Bernard Tschumi, Hani Rashid and Lise Anne Couture (Studio Asymptote), and Toyo Ito among others (in a more modernist vein one must include Jean Nouvel and Jacques Herzog and Pierre de Meuron). Historically, in architecture, the sign or image has been relegated to a secondary, less functional or ornamental role. In the past century in modernism, signification has been subsumed into form and divorced from everyday activities while form (and its idealised use of geometry) has sought transcendence. Pixel or media architecture has sought to bring the vitality of the electronic sign into the surfaces of architecture, but in order to achieve this has negated or neutralised form. This strategy threatens to maintain signification in the role of ornament (see Gary Genosko's response overleaf) and is thus susceptible to commodification. However, media architecture helps to establish an infrastructure for hypersurfaces only without its material aspect. Hypersurface is fully intense when both surface/substance and signification play through each other in a temporal flux. For instance, if we could strip away all the electronic signs in Times Square, we would find a cacophony of material surfaces, each working to maximise the potential readability of the sign. It is this sort of drive, motivated by economic concerns, that differentiates surfaces, and that will propel the surface into the sign, and the sign into the surface. This 'vulgar' impulse exists outside of the discipline of architecture in terms of pure commercialism even though it has been acknowledged in the media architecture trajectory. The media complex (as Paul Virilio continually describes it and how Brian Massumi describe its relations to capitalism) involves an impetus of consumption through distended impulses that emerge from everyday life which are becoming transliterated into global digital networks. This dispersion of data is a body without organs. Information culture is spilling out into the built environment, creating a need for surfaces through which data may traverse (hypersurfaces).

Simultaneously, in architectural design, an unprecedented plasticity of form deriving from computer technology is generating new explorations of form. As a result, there is a general topologising of volume-space into activated surfaces, as can be noticed in the work of a number of leading and highly influential practitioners. This second impulse, from within 'proper' confines of the elite practice of architecture, is the deconstruction of Platonics in architectural form into enfolded, radical deformations. Avant-garde architecture, as it is explored and fostered within the academy and which to an extent defines future trajectories, has moved through a phase of self-critique, an inward interrogation of architecture's historical assumptions motivated by poststructuralism. Topology in architecture comes about due to a shift from an interest in language theories (Derrida) to matter and substance (Deleuze) in its theoretical discourses. The topologising of architectural form may be taken as a state of preparation for the reception of the flow of data as it overspills from contemporary cultural activities. A main effect of this transformation entails interconnectivity and continuity among previously systematised categories of architectural technics and production. The malleability of form and programme influenced by newly available technologies also makes possible the realisation of highly differentiated, topological architecture. The same impulses that bring technology to architecture occur throughout and across every facet of culture. An influx of new digital technology interconnects with other transformations taking place in global economic, social, and scientific practices cultivating fluid, continuous and responsive manifestations of architectural morphogenesis.

Architectural topology is the mutation of form, structure, context and programme into interwoven patterns and complex dynamics. Over the past several years, a design sensibility has unfolded whereby architectural surfaces and the topologising of form are being systematically explored and unfolded into various architectural programmes. Influenced by the inherent temporalities of animation software, augmented reality, computer-aided manufacture and informatics in general, topological 'space' differs from Cartesian space in that it imbricates temporal events-within form. Space then, is no longer a vacuum within which subjects and objects are contained, space is instead transformed into an interconnected, dense web of particularities and singularities better understood as substance or filled space. This nexus also entails more specifically the pervasive deployment of teletechnology within praxis, leading to an usurping of the real (material) and an unintentional dependency on simulation.

While the two impulses – pixel and topological architecture – have been separated categorically, at this juncture, overlaps are emerging as a direct result of respective deterritorialisations and auto-destructurations (clearly evident in the recent work by Coop Himmelb(l)au presented in this volume). The events of overlap mark the beginning of more complex interrelations that may provide an opportunity to explore more rigorous and intense manifestations of Otherness. Hypersurfaces may be significant in

FROM ABOVE: Venturi and Scott Brown Associates, Whitehall Ferry Terminal, Staten Island Ferry, 1997 – rejected proposal for a media surface on ferry terminal water side; Frank O Gehry, Guggenheim Museum, Bilbao, 1993-97; Bernard Tschumi, interior of Video Glass Gallery, Gröninger Museum, Gröningen, The Netherlands, 1990; Freemont Street, electronic arcade in Las Vegas – 2.1 million LEDs connected to a computer animation. This condition equivocates a built surface to a computer screen

the manner in which traditional assumptions are re-routed or are self-configured. Hypersurface is the activation of latent or virtual potential within forming substrates, membranes, surfaces, as an interstitial relation between bodies and objects; each distended as language/substance-matter. This does not occur as an intervention into an existing context, but becomes manifest due to complex interactions between technological manifestations and our media saturated background.

A hypersurface in architecture is elicited by incommensurate relations between form and image. The effects of hypersurface are also Other than that of either form or image. This is not the classical application of image or ornament to form, or the reverse: it is a superposed image, thereby creating a semi-autonomous form (through decontextualisation) and in turn, incompleteness or lack. Both image (programme) and form become part of each other and part of larger and other logics. For example, the presence of an advert on a billboard creates an incompleteness in its connection to a context (as in Guattari's notion of the machinic). Even though a hypersurface is an effect created by an incommensurate form-image relation, this condition creates a continuity and thus promotes a fluidity of interrelationships. When an image of an advert is screened over the form of a bus, the ad-graphic both accepts and denies the bus form. The advert parasitically appropriates the generally readable surface over the side of a bus. But the bus has other qualities that make it a graphically-charged surface, such as mobility. It is a surface that is latent with the potential to pass innumerable readers (willingly or not). The bus can remain fully functional and is unimpeded in having become fully appropriated by this ad-graphic. We may notice that the presence of the advert is connected to the forces of consumption giving the use of this form-surface a commercial value.; a value that is also calculated by the consumablility of the surface. An advert must be brushed-over by reader-bodies to have worth. This is a rudimentary formulation of what may be considered a haptic tangibility, or how the dynamics of consumption lead to such qualities of space.

Architecture configures subjectivity in a process that does not determine either polarity in the traditional subject-object distinction. Instead, we might describe a process that works over and throughout a plane of immanence from the middle-out. In the contemporaneous nexus of culture, human agency is evermore defined through technological interfaces. Subjectivity co-figures architecture in a complex way. This activation of the vitality of a constitutive middle-zone is neither understood solely as architecture nor as subjectivity, as *de facto* determinants in a co-constitutive dynamic. We will need to leave behind the dialectic constructs of habit – a middle-out logic, one of unfolding and enfolding; of proliferative differentiation.

E-mail from Gary Genosko, February, 1998
Dear Stephen, Your critique of dichotomaniac thought by way of the collapse of dominant dualities, which reveals their transversal connections on a plane of immanence, strongly suggests that the dominant generative force is consumer society. This ties hypersurface phenomena to capitalist codes, reinstating a dominant semiology on the plane of immanence and more or less defeating the purpose of your critique. The idea that hypersurfaces produce intensive effects must mean that singular traits of these effects are maintained against capitalist translations of them. This means that a certain amount of a-signifying semiosis must be at work in hypersurfaces: the relation between formal and

material fluxes must in some manner elude capitalist representations of them (if they fail to do so they will cancel each other out). Of course, hypersurface phenomena need to borrow capitalist semiologies, but they also need to retain some autonomy from them. I suppose, all that needs to be admitted is that hypersurface semiotics eludes the dominant meaning-giving formalisms of a signifying regime based on dichotomies, that they cannot be captured as a language (architecture is not a language!). What is hypersurface architecture? Well, it is not a pure signifying semiology, for one thing; it engages semiotic substances that are non-linguistic, especially tactile, which are relatively untranslatable into language, which is one of their virtues; and this tactility cannot be reduced to visual coding.

Response
Dear Gary, I am suggesting that hypersurfaces are an incommensurate complexity conjoined by a number of simultaneous impulses stemming from schizo-culture. One is from a Heideggerian/Derridean trajectory, whereby capitalism brings about a deconstruction and deterritorialisation of subjectivity through its modes of production. This is almost a Walter Benjamin thesis, but one needs post-phenomenology to talk about 'hyper' as flickering signifiers floating through material surfaces. This trajectory is the vulgar culture side and the material part is found in the architecture context, which has led to the topologising of form into surfaces. I think that when these two incommensurates conjoin: hyper-to-surface, they are not aligned, bringing about intensive effects that are not reducible to language. Indeed, they resist such consumptive subsumption, manifesting themselves instead as generative or autopoeitic.

As with a Jackson Pollock painting, there is no possible reduction. It is a field that only opens to greater complexity; a nexus of interweavings. Hypersurfaces result from the messiness of everyone's lines of communication criss-crossing over one another leading to disfiguration, with the architects trying to supply a membrane with which to support such crossings. They never can because the excess of media is too great, thereby contributing to the fluctuation of it all. The entire scene is one of autopoeitic emergence. Like randomly generated noise that has moments of clarity; a productive schizophrenia. Such effects are not reducible to language because they are merely effects that are shifting back and forth between the material and the immaterial; generated by consumption yet not providing a common ground upon which to build a socius. Gary, this is a main point about hypersurfaces: a material/immaterial flux of actual discourse (partially constituted by commerce) that cannot result in a political collectivity. Hypersurfaces are socius fluxus; a transversal of intersubjectivity. No governing consciousness, no material foundations – all middle. Out.

Productive schizophrenia: hypersurfaces from the middle-out
Hypersurface theory involves the simultaneous holding of a Heideggerian effect with a Deleuzean effect. Both conditions have become relevant because of the way culture has unfolded and embraced technology. The two trajectories are somewhat incommensurate: one is phenomenological and one is proprioceptive. This is why hypersurface theory is not a fusion of the two, but a theory that allows for both simultaneously. This is the basis for a productive schizophrenia. This is why an incommensurate effect is now resulting in architecture/culture. How will this schizo-doubling be productive? The strategy within a term like

'hypersurface' is to suggest that architecture is an inhabitable envelopment of between deterritorialised subjects and objects. Deleuze argues that everything is connected prior to divisions, thus subject and matter are fundamentally linked. What is described in this document is the complex of forces that are evacuating the dualisms that have categorically kept subjectivity and materiality apart. They are forces that undermine the tenets of separation and come from the machinations of our everyday life, which is now interconnected by digital teletechnology.

Hypersurface theory acknowledges that prior to experiences with the contemporary built environment, one is already affected by the media complex. This techno-existential condition situates us in an inescapable relation to media (here media meant to be broadly inclusive of all modes of representation in culture that are facilitated by technology). Activity in the contemporary milieu triggers associations that resonate within a partially constructed subject. The co-presence of embodied experience superposed upon mediated subjectivity is a hypersurface. The manifestation of this construct in the built environment is a reflection of this. If we are part-media constructs then it will be manifested in the built environment, an inflected place where we encounter our-selves, but as technology. Hypersurfaces appear in architecture where the co-presence of both material and image upon an architectural surface/membrane/substrate such that neither the materiality nor the image dominates the problematic. Such a construct resonates and destabilises meaning and apprehension, swerving perception transversally into flows and trajectories.

The purpose of hypersurface theory is to describe an emerging phenomenon in architecture and culture as a means to go beyond schizophrenic or nihilistic interpretations that contribute to the dynamics occurring in our complex world today. Prior to the divisions between things, there is a more pervasive connectedness. There are many approaches to this impossibly complex configuration but a few themes may be explored to uncover the underlying dynamics of connection before division. Hypersurface theory suggests an architecture/culture from the middle-out. What is a middle-out architecture and how does it stand in opposition to other theories about architecture? What would it be to think architecture from the middle-out? To what end?

Firstly, it would not be an end. Middle-out works in an alternate way from our more dominant tendency to think of oppositions and privileging one or other entity. This is what we learned from deconstruction: that binary oppositions operate to create frame-works for all that is meaningful. Does this mean that we are interested here in a meaningless architecture? What situation are we confronted with at the beginning of a new millennium?

Hypersurface architecture is the simultaneous and incommen-surate action of human agency over a material topology. A hypersurface is the co-presence of the activities of human agency taking effect in a form-substance of force, or linguistic signifier as it occurs in a plane of immanence relative to another plane of immanence whose form-substance is that of matter. Intensities occur where these two planes of immanence create new planes of immanence – none of which participates in any absolute or transcendental logics. Hypersurface is that condition made possible as a result of the forces effecting both human-becoming and form-matter, such that these two polarities are no longer apposite and isolated. They each instead commingle and proliferate, establishing the rudiments of what may soon become an intersubjective plane of immanence. Mind and body meet in hypersurface in a conjunction with the realm of form-substance

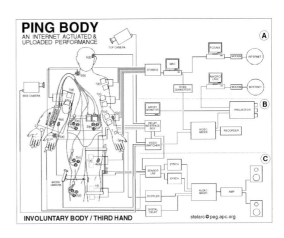

FROM ABOVE: Toyo Ito, Noh Theatre, model, 1987; Stelarc, Ping Body, 1996 – 'pinging' employed as a control mechanism for the body, the Net becoming the external nervous system; Serge Salat, Aleph I, Palais National de la Culture, Sofia, 1989

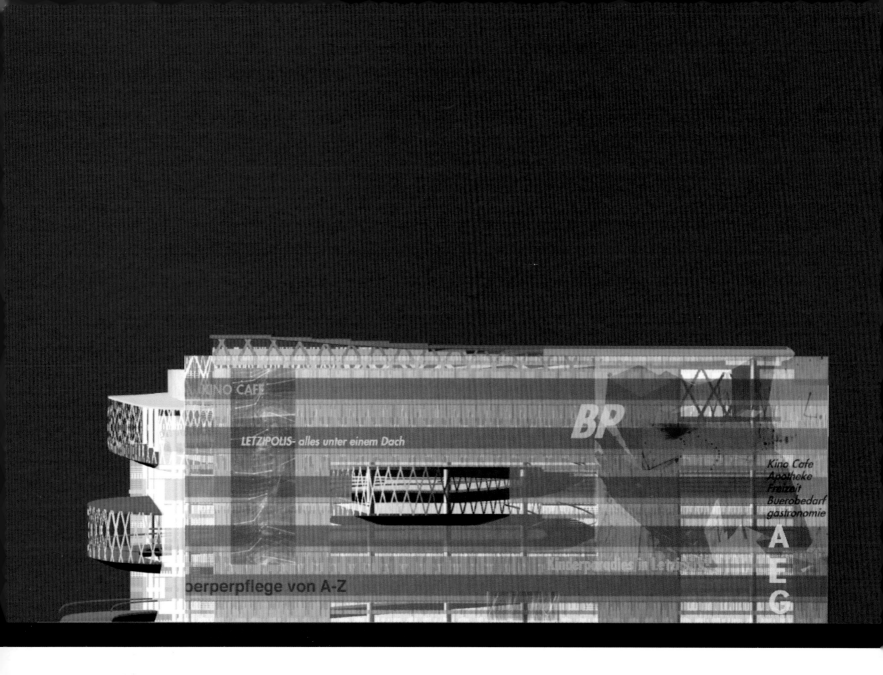

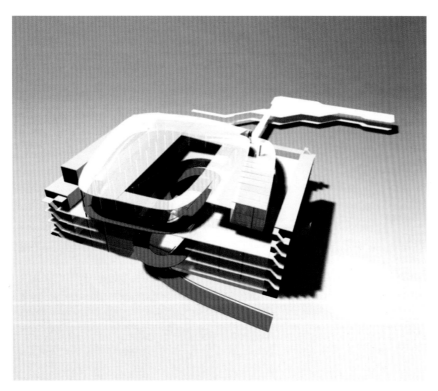

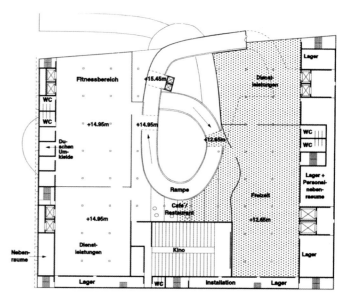

Bernard Tschumi, Zurich Department Store, 1995.
FROM ABOVE, L TO R: Model; computer-generated image;
plan. This competition entry reveals an attempt to express
the dance of consumer-to-object, object-to-consumer

and are let-to-flow as planes of immanence in a hypersurface architecture. Our bodies are hypersurfaces, convex and concave surfaces over and through which sense flows. This is an irreducible condition having neither an absolute inside nor outside.

Inside must reconnect to the outside through imagination, but one that is configured by a highly problematic intersubjectivity. Hypersurface is the activation of those latent potentials within substrates, membranes or surfaces that constitute the interstitial relations between bodies (distended as language) and substance-matter. This does not occur as an intervention into an existing context but becomes manifest due to complex interactions between technological manifestations and our background and past that is latent through having been saturated with the media. The unconscious always exits in the background, underlying human motives, operating just beneath apprehension. Psychoanalytics brings an interpretation of these operations to the surface but not into any full framework of understanding. The effects of hypersurface are beyond that of either form or image. Generally, a hypersurface has a range of effects, including and most significantly a surreality or hyperreality; a realism that is simultaneously uncanny, incomprehensible and therefore a catalyst or provocation, but not in any overt way. Being neither in the context of the purely conscious or unconscious, hypersurfaces slip readily between these realms, in the seam between the two. A hypersurface is the informed topology of an interstitial terrain between the real and unreal (or any other binary opposition) which then flows transversally into a stream of associations. Our current condition of stasis in an audio-visual world is what Virilio means by the 'last vehicle'. But it is a condition that will be overcome as our mediatised sensibilities begin to flood into the new proliferation of architectural forms being transformed into topological hypersurfaces.

Note

1   Quotation from the studio pamphlet developed by Steven Izenour for a studio at Yale University, 1995.

References

John Brockman, *The Third Culture*, Simon & Schuster (New York), 1995.
Hal Foster, *The Return of the Real*, The MIT Press (Cambridge, Mass), 1996.
Denis Hollier, *Against Architecture: The Writings of Georges Bataille*, Betsy Wing (trans), The MIT Press (Cambridge, Mass), 1989.
'Architecture After Geometry', *Architectural Design*, Academy Group Ltd (London) 1997.
Looking Back on the End of the World, Dietmar Kamper, Christoph Wulf (eds), David Antal (trans), Semiotext(e) (New York), 1989.
Todd May, *Reconstructing Difference: Nancy, Derrida, Levinas, and Deleuze*, The Pennsylvania State University Press (University Park), 1997.
Avital Ronell, *The Telephone Book: Technology, Schizophrenia, Electric Speech*, The University of Nebraska Press (Lincoln), 1991.
Immersed in Technology: Art and Virtual Environments, Mary Anne Moser with Douglas MacLeod (eds), The MIT Press (Cambridge, Mass), 1996.
Gilles Deleuze, *The Logic of Sense*, Constantin V Boundas (ed), Mark Lester with Charles Stivale (trans), The Columbia University Press (New York), 1990.
Anne Friedberg, *Window Shopping: Cinema and the Postmodern*, The University of California Press (Berkeley, California), 1993.
Robert Venturi, *Iconography and Electronics Upon a Generic Architecture: A View from the Drafting Room*, The MIT Press (Cambridge, Mass), 1996.
J Abbott Miller, *Dimensional Typography*, Kiosk Report (Princeton), 1996.

Gianni Vattimo, *The End of Modernity*, J R Snyder (trans), The John Hopkins University Press (Baltimore), 1988
Paul Virilio, *The Vision Machine*, Julie Rose (trans), The Indiana University Press (Bloomington), 1994.
Gilles Deleuze, *Cinema 2: The Time-Image*, Hugh Tomlinson and Robert Galeta (trams), The University of Minnesota Press (Minneapolis), 1994.
Gilles Deleuze, *The Fold: Leibniz and the Baroque*, Tom Conley (trans), The University of Minnesota Press (Minneapolis), 1993.
Gilles Deleuze and Félix Guattari, *A Thousand Plateaus: Capitalism and Schizophrenia*, Brian Massumi (trans), The University of Minnesota Press (Minneapolis), 1987.
Bernard Cache, *Earth Moves: The Furnishing of Territories*, Michael Speaks (ed), Anne Boyman (trans), The MIT Press (Cambridge, Mass), 1995.
Brian Massumi, *A User's Guide to Capitalism and Schizophrenia: Deviations from Deleuze and Guattari*, The MIT Press (Cambridge, Mass), 1992.
Tony Fry (ed), *Heidegger and the Televisual*, The Southwood Press (Sydney), 1993.
Félix Guattari, *Chaosmosis: An Ethico-Aesthetic Paradigm*, Paul Bains and Julian Pefanis (trans), The University of Indiana Press (Bloomington), 1995.
Ada Louise Huxtable, *The Unreal America: Architecture and Illusion*, The New Press (New York), 1997.
Gianni Vattimo, *The Transparent Society*, David Webb (trans), The John Hopkins University Press (Baltimore), 1992.
Mark Wigley, *The Architecture of Deconstruction: Derrida's Haunt*, The MIT Press (Cambridge, Massachusetts), 1993.
Mark Wigley, *White Walls, Designer Dresses: The Fashioning of Modern Architecture*, The MIT Press (Cambridge, Mass), 1995.

BRIAN MASSUMI
SENSING THE VIRTUAL, BUILDING THE INSENSIBLE

The 'virtual', it is hard not to notice, has been making a splash in architecture. Its full-blown entry into the discourse was somewhat belated in comparison to other fields. This has been to architecture's great advantage, for the poverty of prevailing conceptions of the virtual, in its popular compound with 'reality', has become all too apparent. 'Virtual reality' has a short conceptual half-life, tending rapidly to degrade into a synonym for 'artificial' or 'simulation', used with tiresome predictability as antonyms for 'reality'. The phrase has shown a pronounced tendency to decompose into an oxymoron. It was in that decomposed state that it became a creature of the press, a death warrant on its usefulness as a conceptual tool.

There is a countervailing tendency to use 'virtual' without the 'reality' tag – not because the virtual is thought to have no reality but because its reality is assumed, the only question being what mode it takes. It is in the work of Gilles Deleuze and Félix Guattari that this current gains its most elaborated contemporary expression. The advantage of architecture is that the virtual has been introduced into its discourse by theorists and practitioners cognisant of the impasse of earlier appropriations of the concept in other domains, and conversant with the alternative Deleuze and Guattari's work represents.

Deleuze and Guattari, following Bergson, suggest that the virtual is the mode of reality implicated in the emergence of new potentials. In other words, its reality is the reality of change: the *event*. This immediately raises a number of problems for any domain of practice interested in seriously entertaining the concept. If the virtual is change as such, then in any actually given circumstance it can only figure as a mode of abstraction, for what is concretely given is what is – which is not what it will be when it changes. The potential of a situation exceeds its actuality. Circumstances self-abstract to the precise extent to which they evolve. This means that the virtual is not contained in any actual form assumed by things or states of things. It runs in the transitions from one form to another.

The abstractness of the virtual has been a challenge to certain discourses, particularly in the interdisciplinary realm of cultural theory, which make a moral or political value of the concrete. This is not the case with architecture, even though its intimacy with the concrete is quite literal. Architecture has always involved, as an integral part of its creative process, the production of abstract spaces from which concrete forms can be drawn. The challenge that the virtual poses for architecture lies more in its 'unform' nature than its abstractness. How can the run of the unform be integrated into a process whose end is still-standing form?

The answer for many has been topology. Topology deals with continuity of transformation. It engulfs forms in their own variation. The variation is bounded by static forms that stand as its beginning and its end, and it can be stopped at any point to yield other still-standing forms. But it is what happens in-between that is the special province of topology. The variation of seamlessly interlinking forms takes precedence over their separation. Forms figure less as self-enclosures than as open co-dependencies of a shared deformational field. The continuity of that field of variation is inseparable from the forms populating it. Yet it exceeds any one of them, running across them all. When the focus shifts to continuity of variation, still-standing form appears as residue of a process of change, from which it stands out (in its stoppage). A still-standing form is then a *sign*: of the passing of a process. The sign does not in the first instance signify anything. But it does imply something; or better, it implicates. It envelops in its stillness a deformational field of which it stands as the trace: at once a monument of its passing and a signpost of its potential to be repeated. The variation, as enveloped past and future in ceasing form, is the virtuality of that form's appearance (and of others with which it is deformationally interlinked).

Topology has exerted a fascination on certain contemporary architects because it renders form dynamic. This has important consequences for both the design process and the built form to which it leads.

The topological turn entails a shift in the very object of the architectural design process. Traditionally, form was thought of as both the raw material and end product of architecture, its origin and telos. Form bracketed design. Approached topologically, the architect's raw material is no longer form but *deformation*. The brackets swing open. Form falls to one side, still standing only at the end. Form *follows* the design process, far from enclosing it. Far from directing it, form *emerges* from the process, derivative of a movement that exceeds it. The formal origin is swept into transition. Followed by architect.

One thing swept away is the popular image of the architect as autonomous creative agent drawing forms from an abstract space of Platonic pre-existence to which he or she has inspired access, and artfully dropping them into the concrete of everyday existence, which is thereby elevated. The architect's activity becomes altogether less heroic – and the abstract more palpable, for the architect must follow the same process that the form follows. The architect becomes a prospector of formative continuity, a tracker in an elusive field of generative deformation. The abstract field of variation takes on a certain post-Platonic thickness, in and by its very elusiveness, by becoming a field of hands-on exploration and experimentation. New form is not conceived. It is coaxed out, flushed from its virtuality. The architect's job is in a sense catalytic, no longer orchestrating.

Le Corbusier outlines the antithetical position in an early manifesto:

> The goal of art is to put the spectator . . . in a state of an elevated order. To conceive, it is first necessary to know what one wishes to do and specify the proposed goal . . . Conception is, in effect, an operation of the mind which foreshadows the general look of the art work . . . Possessed of a method whose elements are like the words of a

language, the creator chooses among these words those that he will group together to create a symphony ... One comes logically to the necessity ... of a logical choice of themes, and the necessity of their association not by deformation, but by formation.[1]

Here, creation consists in the masterful composition of aggregate forms, drawing on a pre-existing vocabulary of combinable elementary forms. Creation is an individual expression of the artist at the same time as it accedes to universality. The 'pure' artist possesses a superior combinatorial logic allowing 'him' to articulate to 'universality' of 'man': a 'capital point, a fixed point'. Forms, in this account, are elementary, and elementary forms are 'words' signifying 'universal' principles of fixity. The completed forms could not be further from the asignifying signs, materially enveloping singular conditions of change and emergence, towards which hands-on topological experimentation moves.

Those hands, of course, are on the computer keyboard. In a most unCADlike way. The computer is not used to prefigure built form, in the sense of presenting an anticipatory image exactly resembling it. The whole point of the topological turn is to catalyse newness and emergence rather than articulating universalised fixation. Of course, topological transformations are just as formalisable, in their own way, as are classical geometric forms. Chance must be added to truly yield change. The computer becomes a tool of indeterminacy. Abstract spaces are no longer neutral screens for imaging what has already been seen in the mind's eye. They must be actively designed to integrate a measure of indeterminacy. As a consequence, the space of abstraction itself becomes active, no longer merely prefiguring. The abstract space of design is now populated by virtual *forces* of deformation, with which the architect must join forces, to which he or she must yield in order to yield newness. The design process takes on a certain autonomy, a life of its own.

From the 'artful genius' perspective, this may seem like a cowardly abdication of creativity to autonomised machinic procedure. In fact, the arbitrary returns. Its first point of re-entry is the way in which the activity of the abstract space is programmed. There is no such thing as pure indeterminacy, certainly not in a programmed environment. Indeterminacy must be designed to emerge from an interplay of constraints. What constraints are set to interact will be an arbitrary decision of the architect, working from a more or less explicitly developed aesthetic orientation, and taking into consideration the functional parameters of the desired end product as well as client preferences on a number of other levels (including cost). The manner in which such 'analogue' traits are translated into topological terms informs the programming, but is not itself preprogrammed. It is the point of entry, into what is nevertheless still an autonomic process, for the architect's decision.

The process does not of itself generate a completed form. It generates a proliferation of forms. The continuity of the deformational

FROM ABOVE: Nox Architects, interior of FreshH$_2$O eXPO (Water Pavilion) – two views; Le Corbusier, Edgar Varése and Iannis Xenakis, Philips Pavilion, 'Poéme Electronique', Brussels World Fair, 1958

variation can be cut at any point, any number of times. The constraints can be tweaked and set in motion again to experimentally generate whole new series of formal separations. The outcome of any given run cannot be predicted. But a choice must be made: a set of forms must be selected to provide the foundation of the actual design. The second area of arbitrariness is in the selection. The overall process is that of an *analogue*. Such constraints as taste, function, preference and cost are analogically translated into virtual forces, which are then set into variation, and analogically translated back into taste, function, preference and cost *as embodied* in the final, composite sign-form. The movement is not from the simplicity of the elementary to the sophistication of the complex. Rather, it is from one arena of complexity to another. Complexes of complexity are analogically launched into interaction. Each complex is separated not by a self-enclosure, but by an analogical gap that the process must leap. The art of the architect is the art of the leap.

Integrating topological procedures involving indeterminacy does not replace creative freedom of expression with machinic necessity. To begin with, the absolutes of 'freedom' and 'necessity' are endemic to the 'creative genius' approach of the Le Corbusier quote. They do not apply to the topological approach, which works instead with arbitrariness and constraint, dosed rather than absolute and locally co-functioning rather than in Promethean struggle with one another as universal principles. The opposition between the absolutes of freedom and necessity was never, of course, itself absolute. The creative freedom enjoyed by the 'purified' artist was predicated on allying himself with a higher necessity (unchanging, universal, 'primary' order). His 'elevated' activity consisted in giving that necessity formal expression in the 'secondary' world of the dirty, ever-changing, individually varying, everyday. The artist separated himself from the every-day in order to return to it, reorder and re-form it. The world itself was his raw material, as if he himself could freely stand outside and against it as pure, formative activity. This elevating mission might be seen as typical of 'high' modernist approaches to cultural production.

To the topologically inclined, things are very different. Arbitrariness and constraint are internal to the process. They are variables among others, in a process that is all variation, and which separates itself into phases, across analogical gaps, instead of separating the 'artist' from the world, the better to impose order upon it. The 'impurities' of the everyday – personal taste, dirty function, preference enforced in part by social convention, and most vulgar of all, cost – enter the process, across the analogic gaps. The translation into and out of virtual force lays everything out on a single, complex, deformational surface from which form emerges as a certain kind of stoppage. The architect's activity is swept up in that complexity, its triggering and stoppage. It works at a level with it. The architect yields dosed measures of his or her activity to the process. The 'arbitrariness' of the decisions that enter and exit the process are more like donations to its autonomy than impositions upon it. Rather than being used to claim freedom for the architect, decision is set free for the process. The architect lets decisions go, and the process runs with them.

'Arbitrariness' might not be the best term for the decisive activity of the architect as process tweaker and form flusher, since that role requires 'following' the process, which in turn requires having a certain 'feel' for its elusiveness, for its running, for its changeability: a feeling for its virtuality. The old and abused term

of 'intuition' perhaps fits better than terms such as arbitrarity, freedom, inspiration, or genius. 'Intuition' is the feeling for potential that comes of drawing close enough to the autonomous dynamic of a variational process to effectively donate a measure of one's activity to it. Intuition is a real interplay of activities. It is neither a touchy-feely dreamlike state nor an imposition from on high of form on matter, order on disorder. It is a pragmatic interplay of activities on a level. The 'donation' involved should not be construed as an 'alienation' of the architect's activity, because what is donated is returned in varied form, ready for insertion into a different process, or a different phase of the same process (building).

None of this has anything to do with purity. Everything is mixed together at the beginning and comes out just as mixed. Constraint enters as conventional strictures and professional expectations, client preference, cost projections, etc. Each of these involves more or less static forms, as well as their own dedicated matters of variation. Arbitrarity or 'freedom' enters in the way those constraints are set into interaction, and how an end-form is extracted from the interaction. That end-form must in some way accommodate itself to these constraints or it will be 'pure' in a very down-to-earth sense: not built. The success of the exercise is not measured by any god-like ability to create something from nothing. It is the more modest ability to extract a difference from a variation (a standing difference from a running variation). It all depends on what happens in the middle. Cultural production becomes the art of the prevailing middle.

This is not really a 'low' modernism against Le Corbusier's 'high' modernism, since it interactivates those categories as well. Neither is it exactly a postmodernism, since the sign-form is primarily a sign of a material differentiation rather than a citation, and it implicates a process rather then referring intertexturally. The architectural activity associated with the topological turn is not unrelated to such modernist adventures as Cage's experiments with chance, or Burroughs' cut-up and fold-in ventures. It might well be considered a neo-modernism, although it has become more acceptable to refer to it, along with its modern antecedents, as neo-Baroque, defined by Deleuze in terms of the 'fold to infinity' (the mutual processual envelopment, on a single abstract variational surface, of complexes of complexity). It mixes procedures evocative of the modern avant-garde with an admitted complicity with vulgar worldly constraints. It might be recalled that Baroque art was an art of patronage. Today's commercial constraints on architecture are different, but just as strong. Maintaining a stance of 'purity' towards them is not a test of political mettle. It is a test of intellectual honesty. It goes without saying that no architect can build without being in complicity with commerce and industry. The choice is not between complicity and purity, but between a politics that maintains the relevance of the distinction and one that recognises that creation in absolute freedom from constraint was only ever a self-aggrandising myth. An architectural politics that admits 'complicity' – the co-functioning of arbitrarity and constraint in the extraction of a standing difference from a running continuity of mixture – is what Deleuze would call an ethics, in distinction to the heroic moralism of the teleologically fixated.

Labels are of limited value. They tend to stereotype, as 'high' modernism inevitably has been in this account for purposes of exposition. The stereotyping can easily extend to both 'sides'. It is just as important not to group too hastily into one rubric all architects who use techniques akin to the ones described here as belonging to the topological turn (as if they constituted a school) as it is to recognise the simplifications that abbreviated accounts like the present one confer upon the topologically challenged. The ways in which the analogical gaps described above are negotiated by architects who are topologically engaged with the virtual will vary widely. There are no constants. The signature engagement with computers is not even necessarily a constant, since allied processual effects may be produced by other means (as the Cage and Burroughs examples indicate). A fluid typology of post-heroic architecture could be delineated along multiple gap-leaping lines of variation, in what may be an expanding field of futurity already prospecting the architectural present (or what may, alternatively, be just a blip). Whatever the fate of contemporary currents, it is more important to multiply productive distinctions than lump camps.

Although the inherited antinomy of freedom and necessity ceases to be the central problem it once was, the topological turn produces ample problems of its own. The originality of a cultural process is measured by the complexity and productiveness of the new problems it creates, not the neatness of its creative solutions; for in complexity there is life. A good problem is a gift of life, the provision of an opening for others' activities, for uptake by other processual dynamisms, a contribution to the collective surface of continuing variation. By that standard, the topological turn in architecture is already a stunning success.

Foremost among the problems it produces is the nature of the actual relation between the built forms that emerge from its process and the process as it happened. In other words, if the idea is to yield to virtuality and bring it out, where is the virtuality in the final product? Precisely what trace of it is left in the concrete form it deposits as its residue? What of emergence is left in the emerged? If the end form is a sign that does not signify, then what does it do and how does it do it? What is the relation of the asignifying sign to its event?

The problem raised is a semiotic one that neither architecture nor current discourses in cultural theory are well equipped to handle. To be appropriate to its field of application, this semiotic problem must be posed in terms of singular potential, material emergence and event, rather than the tried-and-true terms of universal (or at least general) signifying structure and individual decodings or interpretations variously conforming to it.

The difficulty of the problem is that it points to the continuation of the architectural design process outside of itself, in another process. The outside of architectural design is in a very real sense its own product – the building itself: the life of the building. The building is the processual end of the architectural process, but since it is an end that animates the process all along, it is an immanent end. Its finality is that of a threshold that belongs integrally to the process, but whose crossing is also where the process ceases, to be taken up by other processes endowing the design with an afterlife. The most obvious after-processes are two: looking and dwelling. The exterior of the building takes its place as an object in the cultural landscape, becoming an unavoidable monument in the visual experience of all or most of the inhabitants of its locale. And the building becomes an experienced form of interiority for the minority of those people who live in it, work in it, or otherwise pass through it.

There is resistance from many quarters in architectural discourse to highlighting the experience of the built form. There are very good reasons for this reluctance. Talking about it in signifying semiotic terms of decoding and interpretation clamps the

brackets closed again. It re-imprisons the architectural process in pre-existing formal structure, consigning it to intertextural referral, for those who are familiar enough with and care enough about the collective conventions, or to the banality of metaphorical 'free' association on the part of those operating 'below' the structural level of citation, on the local level of 'individualised' variation. The latter is, in fact, entirely prepackaged, since all of the 'individual' variations pre-exist as possible permutations of the general structure of signification. The variation is punctual. It does not emerge. It is 'realised' (conceived) at structurally spaced intervals, at predictable 'positions'. In the end, there really is not such a great a difference between the self-conscious structural irony of the citationalists and the heartfelt 'personal' metaphors of 'naive' associationists. The uptake has been into a process that assumes an opposition between the constant and the variable, and can therefore hope, at best, to achieve a sterile dialectical synthesis between imposed form and 'freely' chosen pre-authorised variations ('discovery' deconstructively unmasked as 'really' being a 'reading'). Quite different is continual variation, in which everything enters the mix and in which there are no constants (even though things may occasionally stand still) and no structural pre-existence (even if there is ample systemic feedback), and thus neither dialectic nor deconstruction (only deformation and emergence). This is the true alienation: when the immanent outside is not only taken up but is taken away by a process so legibly alien to it.

Another receiving-end option is phenomenological. The way of phenomenology posits a 'raw', unprepackaged substrate still perceptible, if only one knows how to 'return' to it, beneath the structure of referral and association. The substrate is construed as 'intentional', or as prefiguring subject-object relations. The experiential substrate, it turns out, is not so much unprepackaged as it is packaged by a structural pre-fit between the body and the world. This has the merits of avoiding imprisonment in signification, and of reconnecting with material processuality. But it consigns everything to function, hypostasised as the ontological ground of lived experience. 'Intentionality' is another word for function, glorified as the ground of all experience. This transcendentalisation of function encloses process in organic form; another difference between 'high' modernism and existential phenomenology, although not so great as it is made out to be. For both, experience is formally prefigured.

The difference is that in the first case the form is purely, otherworldly geometric, and in the second, rawly organic, 'lived' and at one with the world (the world made flesh). The great rallying cry of Deleuze's view of creativity, as a drawing on the virtuality of process by a yielding to it, is the Spinozan slogan that 'we do not know what a body can do'. Phenomenology cannot yield (to) the virtual, whose 'body' is emphatically 'machinic': an autonomised processuality (if not necessarily a high-tech one). It cannot take the machinic indeterminacy of the virtual, even when it takes its own topological turn (as in Merleau-Ponty's last work on folding and gapping, or 'chiasmus').[2] It cannot step over that threshold. It can only stand a 'return' to the well-trodden ground of possibilities for organic functioning. The divergence between Deleuze and phenomenology is summed up in another slogan: to the phenomenologists, 'consciousness is always *of* something' (cognitive prefit).[3] Deleuze responds, 'consciousness always *is* something' (ontological emergence).

The topological turn in architecture must avoid both these directions, and does. But does it live up to the project of drawing on the virtual to draw out the new? The question remains: how could it if its end product is still recognisably standing form? By virtual definition, the built form does not resemble its conditions of emergence. It does not resemble the virtual forces generating it, or the analogical gaps its generation leaps. Unlike a structure of constants and variable realisations of it, the asignifying sign-form does not conform to its own event: there can be no conformity between the product and its process, no one-to-one correspondence between end result's formal features and the steps of its deformational emergence. Virtuality cannot be seen in the form that emerges from it. The virtual gives form, but itself has none (being the unform of transition). The virtual is impercep-tible. It is insensible. A building is anything but that. A building is most concrete.

This impasse has led to the frequent complaint that the architecture operating in the topological field is formally indistin-guishable from modernism: that there is nothing so 'original' about it, nothing to it but a lot of techno-tricks in the design process that leave no visible trace in the built form, at least none that anyone not directly involved in the design could be expected to notice or care about. Isn't it still a building, to which a style can be attributed, that is recognisable as belonging to a particular category of building, that fulfils the typical functions of its kind? Where is the newness? In the computer gadgetry? In slight variations on existing architectural themes?

There is no way of effectively responding to this criticism as long as there is no serious attention given to the afterlife of the design process in the life of the building. Taking the looked-at, lived-in life of the building into account does not fatally entail a surrender to the structural reduction of the signifying sign, or to the phenomenological apotheosis of organic form and function. There is, perhaps, a way out of the impasse, but only if there is a willingness to reentertain questions about perception, experi-ence and even consciousness that have, for some time now, been anathema to many in architecture, as well as in other domains of cultural theory and production.

Although the virtual, Deleuze explains, cannot itself be seen or felt, it cannot not be seen or felt, as other than itself. What he means is that in addition to residue in static form, the formative process leaves traces still bearing the sign of its transitional nature. These are not virtualities, but populations of actual effects that more fully implicate changeability and the potential for further emergence than self-enclosed forms or ordered agglomerations of forms realising a rigid combinatory logic to produce citations, associations, or most ubiquitously, stock functional cues – formal compositions following laws of perspec-tive and resemblance designed to awaken habitual patterns of recognition and response. In even the most ordered formal composition there are accident zones where unplanned effects arise. Nonperspectival, unresembling, they are just glimpsed, in passing, as anomalies in the planned interrelation between actual forms. They are surprising, perhaps mildly disorientating; sometimes, just sometimes, shocking. They are less perceived than side-perceived; half-felt, like a barely palpable breeze; half-seen, on the periphery of habitual vision. They are *fogs* or *dopplerings*; patches of vagueness or blurrings presenting to the senses an insensible plasticity of form; flushes of freshness, arun in concretised convention and habit; recalls of emergence, reminiscences of newness.

Fogs: actual traces of the virtual are often light effects. Although we tend to think of the perceptual dimensions of light as clearly distinguishable and almost boringly familiar, they are not so docile on closer inspection. Experimental psychology, even after decades of trying, is still at great pains to set even the most 'obvious' boundaries between different light-related phenomena. What is the relation of white and black to lightness and darkness? Are the shades lying in a continuum between those extremes shadows or achromatic colours, intensities of light or gradations of grey? How can the distinction between chromatic and achro-matic colours be maintained in the face of such everyday effects as the coloured shadows so lovingly catalogued by Goethe? Is there a simple relation between colour, light intensity, and illumination? Where for that matter is the boundary between one colour of the familiar spectrum and another? What sets the boundary between glimmer, white and clear? How do reflectance and translucence enter into the equation?[4] The boundaries we set and distinctions we function by are habitual. According to many theorists of vision, they do not replace the infinitely complex perceptual fog that is our originary and abiding experi-ence of light. They occur with them, alongside, in a parallel current or on a superposed abstract perceptual surface, in a perpetual state of emergence from the continuum of light dimen-sions that one frustrated would-be tamer of visual anomaly termed 'the brightness confound'.[5]

The 'brightness confound' can become a conscious percept, through a concerted effort of unlearning habits of seeing, or through a simple accident of attention. When it does, the confound is contagious. It strikes depth: three dimensionality, argues the 'ecological' school of perceptual theory,[6] is an effect of complex differentials of surface lighting played out in ever-shifting proximities of shadow and colour, reflectance and lumi-nosity, illumination and translucence (it is not, as traditional theories of perception would have it, the product of mysterious calculations of relative size and distance).

Depth is a surface effect susceptible to the brightness con-found. When it goes, so does separable form. Not only do the relative size and distance of objects flutter, their boundaries blur. They cease to be separate figures, becoming not entirely localisable zones in a fuzzy continuum. In other words, they cease to be objects, becoming what they always were, in the beginning and in parallel: fluctuations; visual runs; experiential transition zones. The distinctions of habit fold back into the always accompanying level of the more-than-three-dimensioned light concurrence from which they emerged. The fixed boundaries and 'constants' of our habitual perceptions are emergences from an experiential con-found to which they can return, and must return, for they are not structural constants at all, but continually regenerated effects, predicated on the variation they follow and emerge from, as its perceptual arrest. They rest entirely on variation.

Architecture, Deleuze will say for this reason, is a distribution of light before it is a concretion of forms.[7] Its basic medium is light. It uses concrete and stone, metal and glass, to sculpt light in ways that either direct the fixations of attention steadfastly away from their confounded conditions of emergence, or on the contrary enable it sporadically to fold-back into them. The separation between 'primary' sensations (ie depth and forms) and 'secondary' sensations (in particular colour and lighting) is untenable. Since perception is a matter of complexes of com-plexities played out in surface relations, the more useful distinc-tions are, again, topological (cuts and continua; boundaries and transitions; fold-outs and fold-backs) and processual (aflutter or stabilised; arun or still-standing; refreshed or habitual; functional or eventful). One of the direct implications for architectural practice is that colour need not be dismissed as essentially decorative. As a dimension of the brightness confound, it is as primary an architectural element as the cube – if not more so.

Dopplerings: actual traces of the virtual are always effects of movement. When it was said that the separations between the perceptual dimensions of light were habitual, what that really meant is that they arise from movement. Depth perception is a habit of movement. When we see one object at a distance behind another, what we are seeing is in a very real sense our own body's potential to move between the objects or to touch them in succession. We are not using our eyes as organs of sight, if by sight we mean the cognitive operation of detecting and calculating forms at a distance. We are using our eyes as proprioceptors and feelers. Seeing at a distance is a virtual proximity: a direct, unmediated experience of potential orientings and touches on an abstract surface combining pastness and futurity. Vision envelops proprioception and tactility, by virtue of past multi-sense con-junctions whose potential for future repetition our body immediately, habitually 'knows', without having to calculate. Seeing is never separate from other sense modalities. It is by nature synaesthetic, and synaesthesia is by nature kinaesthetic. Every look reactivates a multi-dimensioned, shifting surface of experience from which cognitive functions emerge habitually but which is not reducible to them. It is on that abstract surface of movement that we 'live' and locate. We cannot properly be said to see, or experience, three-dimensional space and the bounded forms filling it. Rather, it is they that emerge from the abstract surface of experience, as reductive concretions and relative stoppages of it. Our seeing *stops* with perspective and form. We do not see or experience perspectival forms from the outside: they occur to our experience and in it, as arrest events that befall it. We ourselves – as spatially located forms in regular interaction with other forms, as embodied subjects in reciprocity with objects – must be co-occurrences with depth and boundary, co-emergences of con-cretion and stoppage, companion arrests, fall-out of the befallen. 'We' ourselves are stoppage events in the flow of experience.

The relation between space and movement must be inverted, along with the relation between form and lighting. When the relation between space and movement inverts, so does the relation between ourselves and our experience. Experience is no longer in us. We emerge from experience. We do not move through experience. The movement of experience stops with us and no sooner folds back on itself. It continues, alongside us, in parallel: doubling, as a superposed abstract surface in repeated interaction or intersection with the stoppage we have been. Our existence is an ongoing topological transformation of a complexifying abstract ontological surface: separation, fold-back, doubling, intersection, re-separation, fold-back over again, redoubling, resection . . . confound it.

The confound of light envelops form, and with form it envelops space, at which point everything becomes movement. Didn't Bergson argue in the first chapter of *Matter and Memory* that we are beings of light, effects of its differential movements? That our bodies, or for that matter all of matter, are interactions of light with surface dimensions of itself? That the 'abstract surface' is light in itself, interacting infinitely and absolutely with itself, registering or 'feeling' its own variations as form-effects? Con-temporary physics would not disagree.[8]

This essay began with the maxim that the virtuality or change-ability of a form exceeds its actuality. The point of the detour

FROM ABOVE: Jean Dubuffet, Villa Falbala, 1969-73, exterior and interior views; Alvar Aalto, Finnish Pavilion, New York World's Fair, 1939; Frank Stella, Hooloomooloo, *1994, acrylic on canvas*

through the existential brightness confound is that if we apply that maxim to our own life forms, our 'experience' onto-topologically exceeds our being. Experience is our virtual reality. It is not something we have. It is a transformability that has us, and keeps on running with us no matter how hard we try to stand still and no matter how concretely we build. It is our continual variation. Our becoming. Our event: the lightning whose thunder we are.

The suggestion here is that the philosophical correlation of the topological turn in architecture is the idea that the streaming of experience exceeds being; or put another way, that feeling conveys potential and change (the corollary being that the feeling is absolute, or that it is immanent only to its own process: the feeling in and of itself of a matter of variation, emergent stabilities of form effectively aside). This philosophical orientation was dubbed a 'radical' empiricism by William James, and a 'superior' empiricism by Deleuze. What it means for architecture and other plastic arts is that they can rejoin the virtual and take experience into account in the same move.

For architecture to rejoin the virtual and take experience into account in the same move would mean its aspiring to *build the insensible*. If in any composition of forms, however rigid, an accident of attention can return experience to its confound, then it must be possible to make a project of building in just such accidents of attention. In other words, built form could be designed to make the 'accidental' a necessary part of the experience of looking at it or dwelling in it. The building would not be considered an end-form so much as a beginning of a new process. Stable forms can be designed to interact dynamically, as bodies move past or through them singly or in crowds, or as sounds mute or reverberate, or as relations of surface and volume change with the time of day or season, or as materials change state with levels of moisture or temperature, or as the connection between inside and outside varies as an overall effect of these variations in concert with the rhythms of activity pulsing the city or countryside as a whole. Forms can be composed to operate as catalysts for perceptual events returning experience to its confound. A building can harbour foci of implicative vagueness, lucid blurs, dark shimmerings, not-quite things half-glimpsed like the passing of a shadow on the periphery of vision. Architecture can locally and sporadically return experience to that part of itself which can never be perceived as being (since it has only becoming) but cannot but be felt (in passing). Architecture can accept as part of its aim the form-bound catalysis of the unform (the deform).

The vagaries in question here have to do neither with *trompe l'œil*, optical illusion, nor ambiguity. *Trompe l'œil* is fully subordinated to formal resemblance. More distorted (anamorphic) or unanchored practices of simulation play on resemblance, but in needing it to play on, hold fast to it.[9] Optical illusion also never leaves the formal level, being an oscillation between two forms, rather than a rhythm of recursion between form and the unform. Ambiguity, for its part, belongs to signifying structure. It is nothing new for architects to build-in ambiguity in order to make an event of standing form. But ambiguity still addresses the conventional function of the sign-form. It activates citation and association in order to push them towards a critical reappraisal. It operates on the level of conventional sign-form in order to deliver it to critique. Building-in ambiguity may succeed in catalysing an event – but the event is still a meaning event.

The asignifying or processual sign-form of the onto-topological turn catalyses experiential potential rather than meaning. It is a sign of material dynamics of variation, pointing in two directions at once. On the one hand, it recalls the elements of indeterminacy and chance of the design process itself. It is an echo of the experimentations of the architect. But it does not resemble or in any way conform to them. Rather than referring explicitly to them, it refers them to another process. The architect's processual engagement with the virtual is taken up in an alien process: the life of the building, the looking and dwelling of those who pass by it or through it. This process continues from the design process' point of cessation. The virtual is fed forward into the final form. But in final form, the way the potential is yielded (to) bears no resemblance to what befell during the design process, from which, it must be remembered, it is separated by analogical gaps. The feed-forward of virtuality delineates a continuity, but it is a leaping continuity of differentiation. The architect, who donated his or her activity to the autonomisation of a process, now lets the product go, into another process. Architecture is a gift of product for process, the sign-form fundamentally means nothing. It is meant to stand at the threshold between processes. The middle prevails.

The aim of onto-topological architecture has no end. The aim may nevertheless involve many ends: critical, citational, associational, functional, profit-making. In fact, it necessarily involves all of these: it involves them with each other. It adds them to the catalytic mix. Like stability of form, pre-operative conventional sign systems feature as constraints added to the complex mix out of whose interaction the new re-arises in the design product. The aim of processual architecture does not stop at any end. It takes everything from the middle again. The product is re-process.

Although there is no formal resemblance between the re-process in which the product is taken up and the process that produced it, there is a certain correspondence between them. Were there not, the leap across the processual gaps would not earn the name 'analogical'. The correspondence in question does not concern the nature of the forms in play, or even the qualities of the event they mix to make. The correspondence is a processual retake. It is the process of generating the new from an intuitive interplay of constraints and the arbitrary that keeps the continuity across the leaps. The correspondence pertains to the conditions of emergence rather than the actuality of the emerged. In other words, it is virtual. The identity stretched analogically across the gaps of differentiation is 'machinic': what is repeated is autonomisation, same process, different at every take.

Philosophy and architecture have always been on intimate terms: from Plato's city of the republic to Augustine's city of god to Leibniz's monad-house to Heidegger's house of being to Virilio's bunkers, to name just a few. Formalist modernism's high-moral attachment to purity and geometric harmony can only be understood as a concerted philosophical sortie waged through architectural means. Conversely, architectural achievements have often stood as exemplars for philosophy. Architecture flourishes with philosophical infusions; philosophy exemplifies in monuments. Architecture and philosophy are drawn towards abstract-concrete symbiosis with each other (which of these contributes more of the abstract, and which more of the concrete, is not as straightforward as it may seem).

The basic question of this essay has been: what philosophy can or might enter into a symbiosis with architectures engaging with the virtual, in particular by topological means? The answer seems to lie in a 'radical' or 'superior' empiricism. For architecture, the effect of such a symbiosis is a willingness to bring into even more pronounced expression its processual dimensions. That in turn means theoretically and experimentally re-evaluating the separation between the 'primaries' of form and depth and 'secondaries' such as colour and illumination. That further entails an inversion in what is traditionally assumed to be the relation of form and movement, subject-object structurings and experience, constancy and variation. Where it all leads is to a semiotic of singular potential, material emergence, and event: a semiotic for which the abstract is really material, and the sign-form's material

appearance is not only seen. Vision, following this path, must be grasped as inhabited directly by the other senses, and the other senses by vision. In such an asignifying semiotic, all perception figures as synaesthetic, and synaesthesia is seen as a creature of movement. Perhaps most controversially, a distinction is maintained between movements in the actual world between fixed forms, and the absolute movement of process self-feeling, from which the world itself emerges. A tall order. A tall, autopoietic order. But the theory is not without precedents, and the experimentations have palpably begun.

Note on tunnelling to the future

Most palpably, this has begun in the integration of digital technology into architecture. Although computerisation is not a necessary condition for topological experimentation in design, its forecast integration into built form may bring us to a new threshold in the sensing of the virtual in built form or the building of the insensible. Proponents of 'ubiquitous computing' look to the day when digital media becomes architectural: no longer furnishings or infrastructure, but an absolutely integral part of the building. When the digital display becomes as structural architecturally as a window, looking and dwelling will be transformed, but not as completely as when digital media learns to forego the display and the analogy of the window and the interface is able to go anywhere, responding no longer only to mouse- or keystrokes anchored to the screen but to gestures, movements and sounds – dedicated, roving or ambient, compounded or uncompounded with visions and information.

Electronic media offers, in principle if not yet in practice, an infinite connectibility of spaces. It is crucial to be clear about this: it is not the abstract informational content of what the media might connectively deliver, or even the abstract space of the 'infosphere' from which it is drawn, that is virtual. Although the virtual is a mode of abstraction, the converse is not true. Abstraction is not necessarily virtual. It was argued earlier that the possible (or the permutational: encompassing information no less than signification) and the simulated (of which trompe l'œil and anamorphosis are the simplest examples) are abstract without being virtual: the first because it pertains to a generative matrix whose actual permutations pre-exist in it; the second because it retains in one way or another a fundamental link to formal resemblance. What is virtual is the connectibility: potential (the reality of change). It cannot be overemphasised that the virtual is less the connection itself than its -ibility.

The assumption is often made that increasing the sheer number and variety of media connections between locations constitutes a virtualisation. This is to confuse the virtual with the technological thing. If the virtual is not the informational content or its infosphere, neither is it the physical implantation of technology. The distinction between the virtual and technological actualisation is paramount. Comparing two qualitatively different ways of digitally connecting spaces brings out the distinction. 'Windowing' is one. Windowing provides a framed and tamed static perspective from one local space onto another that remains structurally distinct from it. The connection established is predominantly visual, or at most audio-visual. Features from, or of, one locale are 'delivered' into another as information, pre-packaged for local understanding and use. Windowing is communicational. What characterises communication is that it is designed to be 'transparent': no conversion is supposed to take

place by virtue of the connection in and of itself. The receiver must be primed to enable the information to make a difference – to interpret or exploit it. Information is a feed. Neutral packets ('data') are consumed on one side of the window (or screen) to feed a process already understood and under way, with known effect and intent. Nothing new. What is on the other side of the window stays on the other side, and is not affected by the consumptive conversion operated on the delivery side. The 'conversion' is not really a qualitative change because it just augments something already primed and in place there. The connection is segregated from the conversion.

It is for this reason that communcation is termed a mediation or 'transaction' (rather than an action). Whether communication ever really lives up to its transparent aspirations is doubtful. But that is not so much the issue here. The issue at hand is rather to think of another way of connecting spaces that doesn't even make the pretence. Call it 'tunnelling'. Tunnelling cuts directly into the fabric of local space, presenting perceptions originating at a distance. Not data pre-packagings: perceptions. The perceptual cut-ins irrupt locally, producing a fusional tension between the close at hand and the far removed. As the distant cuts in, the local folds out. This two-way dynamic produces interference, which tends to express itself synaesthetically, as the body returns vision and hearing to tactility and proprioception in an attempt to register and respond to a structural indeterminacy. Vision and hearing are transduced into other bodily modes of activation. Tunnelling is not communicational, but transductive. The connection is unmediatedly a conversion. As a consequence, it takes on a thickness of its own. It is not just a transparent delivery. It is something, and its something is a doing: a direct conversion; a qualitative change. Something is happening here: action. But is it here? It is not only bodily modes that transduce. Space itself is converted, from the local-or-distant into a nonlocal. Distant cut-in, local fold-out: the irruptive perceptions retain as much 'thereness' as they take on 'hereness'. Distance as such is directly presented, embodied in local interference. Two-way movement, between near and far. Between: unplaceably in the midst.

Architecturally speaking, tunnelling builds in the prevailing middle of the experiential confound. It makes structural the transductive irruption of the structurally indeterminate. The opposition between the structural or formal and the accidental is disabled. The 'fogs' and 'dopplerings' described above are no longer peripheral and adventitious. The periphery becomes central, the adventitious of the essence. Structure opens onto the potential of the not-yet known or intended. Melding connection with conversion, tunnelling builds in-ibility. The opening is not onto 'the' new: like a new thing. It is onto newness: the reality of transition, the being of the new, quite apart from anything new. Tunnelling may still yield information and function, interpretation and opportunity to exploit in the service of the augmentation of the already-here, or perhaps its purposeful growth into some-*thing* new, but it does so in a second phase – after a second conversion: when its interfering stills and the newness settle into things. Settle it will, but first it stirs, unforms; any information-function or even invention that emerges from the unforming, singed or tinged by it, as by the lightning its thunder was.

Since tunnelling catalyses unform conditions of actual emergence, it must be considered ontogenetic. The connection is an onto-topological cut-in/fold-out that builds in a phase-space of indeterminate potential. The potential cut of the distant into the out-folding local can actually combine with communicational deliveries or in-foldings from the 'infosphere', paradoxically expanding the confound itself to include information as such (if not function, which always follows the unform). The only proviso is that the materiality of the signs encoding the information stands out. In other words, that the signs be as insistently blips of light as they are letters, as insistently sound-wave as voice: forces of perception. When the communicational medium ceases to be transparent and perforce stands out in its materiality, information blends into perception. Information then precedes its under-standing: it is *experienced* as a dimension of the confound before being understood and used and perhaps lending itself to invention. The understanding and use are then already a repetition. Of something they were, but emerged from, diverged from, with no resemblance: transductive perceptual forces, forced *-iblity*, necessarily sensed virtuality. Information takes on a genetic relation to its confounded and *in situ* self. This is a far cry from communication but it may still be considered citational. Tunnelling information builds in what might be called a vertical mode of citationality, in which the citation has a different ontological status from that which is cited, as emergent actuality to repotentialising confound. The relation of the citation to the cited is asignifying and direct, if divergent. The connection between them is processual, more fundamentally experiential than it is cognitive or functional (which are what the experience becomes when it self-diverges).

This kind of self-differing citationality could do with a name to distinguish it from the 'horizontal' postmodern version, in which everything has already been said (delivered) out there some-where, and delivering it again over here only leads to the conclusion that nothing new has happened, only repetition (no matter how many new inventions have hit the market in the meantime). The name 'self-referentiality' will do as well as any for the emergent or becoming version, in which something does occur, or 'recur'. 'Recursion' might be a better word than 'repetition', for what happens to information in the process (re-emergence, renewal, tinging with potential). Information transductively 'recurs', across a 'vertical' or *in situ* distance from

itself (a concretely abstract self-distance, or self-emergent nonlocality). A new arena of self-referential artistic activity calling itself 'relational architecture', developing under the influence of figures like Stelarc who set up transductive linkages between the body and the Internet, experiments with this kind of recursive confounding of informed experience in the built environment.

Much of what may come of these experimentations is still the province of science fiction, or at best futurism, but as digital technology develops and slowly integrates with architecture, it may be helpful to keep three points in mind: 1) No technology in itself is virtual or virtualising. It is always possible to window new media, and there will be strong cultural and economic pressures to do so. Windowed, digital technology limits itself to the insufficiently-abstract of communication, falling short of its transductive capacity to concretise the abstract as such, to confoundedly actualise the virtual. Virtuality is a mode (-*ibility*). It is not in the 'what' of the technology (its specifications and implantations) but in the 'how' of its composition with other formations such as architecture (its modal conditioning). 2) The postmodernists were in a way right when they said that nothing ever happens here (or there), because it all happens in the middle. Another way of making the point about the 'how' is to say that newness and new things are not the same. No matter how many inventions there have been, it does not mean that an event or real transition has occurred. If invention grows from a communicational feed, and then gives itself over to communica-tion, qualitative change is neither here nor there. The reality of change is transduction – which may occur with or without invention. And with or without, may be built. 3) What points one and two infer is that technology, while not constituting change in itself, can be a powerful conditioner of change, depending on its composition or how it integrates into the built environment.

Technically, the 'tunnellings' somewhat futuristically evoked here as actualisations of the reality of change require fibre optics. It is no surprise to the Bergsonian that the actualisation of the virtual in built form rides on waves of light. The metaphysical assertion that our body and matter itself is constituted by light interacting infinitely with itself as its own hyperabstract surface, feeling absolutely its own variations, has little or no importance in itself. It can, however, act as a reminder: to bring it all back to perception: to perception understood positively as actually pro-ductive of existence, or as virtually preceding existing separa-tions of form; to perception in continuity with the world (unform). The reminder is: do not content yourself with facile negative formulations such as 'distance has been abolished', or with structural descriptions of how already-constituted forms in already-separated spaces technically, even inventively, commu-nicate. Bring it all back: to the abstract concretely. Confound it: transduce it.

Notes

1 Le Corbusier and Amédée Ozenfant, 'Purism' (1920), *Modern Artists on Art*, RL Herbert (ed), Prentice-Hall (Englewood Cliffs, NJ), 1964, p62, pp65-67.

2 Maurice Merleau-Ponty, *The Visible and the Invisible*, Alphonso Lingis (trans), Northwestern University Press (Evanston, Ill), 1968.

3 Maurice Merleau-Ponty, *The Primacy of Perception*, James Edie (trans), Northwestern University Press (Evanston, Ill), 1964, p164.

4 The classic treatise on the perceptual vagaries of light is Johann Wolfgang von Goethe, *Theory of Colours*, Charles Lock Eastlake (trans), MIT Press (Cambridge, Mass), 1970. See also Ludwig Wittgenstein, *Remarks on Colour*, Linda L McAlister and Margarate Schättle (trans), Basil Blackwell (Oxford), 1978. See also Jonathan Westphal's gloss, *Colour: Some Philosophical Problems from Wittgenstein*, Aristotelian Society Series, vol 7, Basil Blackwell (Oxford), 1987.

5 Marc H Bornstein, 'Chromatic Vision in Infancy', *Advances in Child Develop-ment and Behavior*, vol 12, Hayne W Reese and Lewis P Lipsitt (eds), Academic Press (New York) 1978, p132.

6 James J Gibson, *The Ecological Approach to Visual Perception*, Houghton Mifflin (Boston), 1979.

7 Gilles Deleuze, *Foucault*, Paul Bové (trans), Minnesota Press (University of Minneapolis), 1986, p57.

8 In relativity theory, 'it is the light figure that imposes its conditions on the rigid figure.' Henri Bergson, *Durée et simultanéité*, PUF (Paris), 1968, p126. See the discussion in Deleuze, *Cinema 1: The Movement-Image*, Hugh Tomlinson and Barbara Habberjam (trans), Minnesota Press (University of Minneapolis), pp8-61. 'Einstein proposed that the particulate nature of matter may be explicable as concentrations and knots in a fundamental, continuous field', David Bohm and F David Peat, *Science, Order and Creativity*, Routledge (London), 1987, p73. 'Blocs of space-time [whose topological torsions constitute rigid bodies] are figures of light', Deleuze, p60.

Shusaku Arakawa and Madeline Gins,
Interaction House, 1997 – 'Body Proper +
Architectural Surround = Architectural
Body'. In this particular project the radical
theorisation of both body and environ and
their interrelations as architectural body are
significant for hypersurface theory. This
project is unique in the artists' oeuvre in its
absorption of everyday media graphics, a
reference to the world of teletechnology, as
it plays over the surface of a doubled and
fragmented labyrinth, a reference also to
language. The rigour of inquiry into both the
graphical and material manifestations creates
the possibility for an interplay between the
graphics and surfaces, creating a plane of
immanence – a hypersurface.

MICHAEL SPEAKS
IT'S OUT THERE...
The Formal Limits of The American Avant-Garde

In an essay published last year, I proposed that a new image of architecture has begun to develop in The Netherlands.[1] This image, I suggested, is one whose Dutchness is fixed neither by national or professional identity, nor by ideology, but instead identifies a disposition towards the artificial urban milieu that today is The Netherlands but which is fast becoming the rest of the world. I went on to suggest that this new urban disposition defines what is fresh and exciting about an emergent generation of Dutch architects, and moreover, that it is what distinguishes them from their North American and European counterparts.

Two features of this urban disposition were identified. The first is a de-emphasis on form development and a renewed focus on the analysis and manipulation of material and immaterial processes such as those recognised by the Rotterdam Maaskant Prize jury in 1996: 'Rotterdam harbour is a particularly instructive and inspiring example of a "modern" environment, of a space whose organization is not so much dictated by traditional planning and urban design concepts as by the rapid and creative management and steering of trends, movements and forces in the field of transport and communication.'[2]

The second feature of this new disposition is a post-avant-garde attitude, which I named 'just there' modernism, after Joost Meuwissen of One Architecture, in Amsterdam. In the same essay, I focused especially on the implications of 'just there': on the banal, everyday reality at hand, and the way that reality is intensified and made to become something else, something unexpected, something new. 'Just there,' I suggested, focuses on the limitations and constraints that architecture necessarily transforms into conditions of possibility. 'Just there' is thus always connected to what cannot be 'just there': to what shapes what is 'just there', and more importantly, what also offers the potential that any architecture must exploit in order to transform what is 'just there' into something else ... even if only by a thread, 'just there' is always connected to what is 'out there'. This was not only implicit in my previous essay, but it is what I meant to suggest by focusing on the 'urban disposition' of these fresh young Dutch architectural offices; for, in the words of a famous contemporary Dutch architect, it is this that allows them to irrigate their architectural intentions.

In what follows, I wish instead to focus on the contemporary American equivalent of these Dutch architects. However, as will become clear there is no such equivalent, for while the Dutch have moved beyond the constraints of the avant-garde, the Americans remain fascinated with its possibilities. Rather than focusing on the connection between what is 'just there' to what is 'out there', however, I wish to suggest that in the most advanced registers of contemporary American architecture there exists a kind of structural condition that makes impossible any connection between the latter. And that is because what is always 'just there' is form. Going from 'just there' to what is 'out there' one is always stopped at the border, thinking it is possible to see beyond it, but what is seen is always defined by this border, by form itself.

Despite our collective boredom with ideology, politics, philosophical truth, and other such accounts of those larger realities which exceed the banality of everyday life, we Americans are nonetheless still interested in what is 'out there', as the popularity of the television series *The X Files* attests. Each episode begins with the teaser, 'the truth is out there'. The implication is that to find it we only have to follow the thread that leads from here to there. With its stylised banality, *The X Files* has set the 'just there' standard for a new inquiry into the vast array of forces that shape the everyday, and it has done so precisely by connecting the leaden normality of town life and petty criminality to paranormal events that make old fashioned conspiracy theory seem small indeed. More importantly, the programme's framing of what is 'out there' is consistent with a number of recent attempts to make the dark, unfathomable chaos lurking just outside our door comprehensible.

The explosion of postmodernist theories in the 80s and complexity theory in the 90s come to mind of course, as well as the now ubiquitous globalisation discourse. However, one of the most interesting, recent expressions of this desire to make comprehensible what is 'out there', is the increasing use of ecological models to explain the relationship between complex, dynamical systems and their environments. Take, for example, Noel Boaz's recently published *Eco Homo*, in which he argues for a climatological account of the emergence of the human species; or economist Alain Lipietz's use of political ecology to put forth a new post-left political agenda. Or the plethora of new management and scenario planning books such as Arie de Geus' *The Living Company* and James F Moore's 'national bestseller', *The Death of Competition*, on whose dust jacket internet guru Esther Dyson writes: 'Moore catches the fundamental shift in business thinking – and behavior – today: the economy is not a mechanism, businesses are not machines. They are co-evolving, unpredictable organisms within a constantly shifting business ecosystem that no one controls.' As the blurb suggests, what is especially appealing about ecological models is not only that they seem to offer a flexible means by which to deal with turbulent environments, but they also offer a way to think of seemingly lifeless, static forms such as corporations, economic communities, or political ideologies, as dynamic, living, changeable life-forms which interact with and alter their environments.

Although our objective is to discuss that life-form otherwise known as architecture, how we do that will depend on whether by architecture we mean a dynamic life-form open to external influences, or a lifeless object on and in which those influences are registered as avant-gardist gestures. It will also depend on what importance we attach to 'the new', whether it is the source of difference and new life or the source of sameness and decrepitude. Reporting on what appeared in 1995 to be renewed architectural interest in the ecological, *Assemblage* profiled two designs entered in the Cardiff Bay Opera House Competition, including Greg Lynn's formally inventive entry,[3] based in part on Gregory Bateson's book, *Steps to an Ecology of Mind*. In its editorial comments, *Assemblage* insists that what is not different or new about this project is its formal strangeness; that is, the fact that it looks so new. What is new, they suggest rather enigmatically, are the projects' 'ecological aspects', realised through '"process studio techniques" tempered by non-automatic generative rules and critiques of the competition brief'. They imply that this is connected to Lynn's interest in the problem of the supple, the fluid, and the body; all, in their view, pre-eminently ecological concerns.

Commenting on some of Lynn's source materials, they in fact remark that Bateson's book, on which Lynn draws, 'is not so much about the science of teratology and the rules for the mutation of form as a search for "an ecology of ideas" that can help us understand "man's relation to his environment"', adding, parenthetically, 'an architectural problem if there ever was one'. So it comes as something of a surprise when they conclude that 'the most amazing, and ultimately most persuasive, thing about these projects is that *nothing has ever looked like this before*'. They qualify this by observing that 'nothing looks different unless it is different and, further, it is virtually impossible to set out intentionally to find a "new look"'.

Perhaps this is so. Perhaps 'this look' and the design techniques used to generate it are part of something different, something new, but *Assemblage* is unable to define what that is. On the contrary, their focus on 'the look' and thus on the formal aspects of the relationship between ecology (understood here as one name for a renewed interest in the relationship between complex systems and their environments) and architecture, while not wrong exactly, does obscure what one might have thought were the real 'ecological aspects' or implications of Lynn's Cardiff Bay Opera House. Namely, that if taken seriously, an ecological disposition would require us to think in a new way not only about the 'ecological', biomorphic look of Lynn's project, but also, and more significantly, about the relationship between his practice of architecture (which includes 'the look' and the techniques used to generate it) and those larger forces external to architecture; as do, for example Reyner Banham's *Los Angeles: Architecture of Four Ecologies*, in which he describes, among other things, the conditions necessary for the emergence of new architectural life, or Rem Koolhaas' proto-ecologistic (in this larger sense) assertion of 'Bigness', that limit beyond which architecture becomes urbanism.

The need to rethink not only architectural forms but the forms of architectural practice becomes even more appropriate when we consider Lynn's accompanying text, 'The Renewed Novelty of Symmetry'. Here, Lynn follows Bateson's model of symmetry breaking as a way to introduce novelty into a system, novelty being the ultimate guarantor of continued existence for evolving life-forms. As Lynn points out, one of the fascinating insights offered by Bateson is that the introduction of novelty leads not to disorganisation but to greater, more complex organisation within the system. Surprisingly, lack of external information leads to a less ordered, less coherent system, which means a less adaptable and thus more susceptible system. When external information is introduced into a system it triggers sets of regulators that prevent default symmetrical arrangements with less organisation; this results in more complex, internally coherent organisation. The point is that diversity and external influence result in more internally coherent and fluid organisational structure. As Lynn writes in his concluding paragraph:

> Symmetry breaking is not a loss but an increase in organization within an open, flexible, and adaptive system. Symmetry breaking from the exact to the anexact is the primary characteristic of supple systems. These flexible economies index the incorporation of generalized external information through the specific unfolding of polymorphic, dynamic, flexible, and adaptive systems. Symmetry is not a sign of underlying order but an indication of a lack of order due to an absence of interaction with larger external forces and environments. Given this complex conceptualization of endogenous and exogenous forces, deep structure and typology are just what they seem to be: suspect, reductive, empty, and bankrupt. An alternative is an internal system of directed indeterminate growth that is differentiated by general and unpredictable external influences, producing emergent, unforeseen, unpredictable dynamic, and novel organizations.[4]

It would seem to require an extraordinary effort to stop at 'the look' when the very nature of these models requires that we move beyond this and think about architecture's relationship to its exterior, namely to the globalised urban world in which it must, as a practice, struggle to survive. Lynn's description of supple systems seems an excellent description of architecture if by that we mean not simply a supple form but a supple form of practice. Indeed, it seems an apt description of a practice such as Lynn's own, which takes in external information, such as the very Batesonian model under discussion, triggering a set of internal regulators which prevent the system from defaulting into a less organised, less adaptable system, inducing instead the emergence of a more complex, adaptable system.

But therein lies the problem: if, as *Assemblage* seems to suggest, it is only 'the look' that is new, then the only means by which Lynn is able to address the complexity of contemporary urban life is through form. All of the quite remarkable things Lynn attributes to supple systems are thus registered only on the forms themselves. The introduction of external information – Bateson – leads in that case not to a more complex organisation, a new practice of architecture able to adapt to this complex world, but only to a defaulted, less organised, system, or practice of architecture as form-producer.

Now it would be unfair to criticise Lynn for not applying this kind of metacritical position to his own work; that is, for not pushing the implications of his supple systems analyses past the form, and the design techniques which create them, to include an analysis of his practice of architecture itself. The same cannot be said for *Assemblage*, however, a magazine that stakes its reputation on its hypercriticality and sensitivity to external conditions. And yet it cannot really be faulted either, for there is a kind of structural condition that prevents *Assemblage* and Greg Lynn from exploiting the real 'ecological aspects' of his project. Despite being pulled out into the exterior of architecture by his stated interest in urbanism, and by theoretical models such as those of Bateson, Lynn is more powerfully drawn back into contemporary American architecture's most powerful interiority: form. And strange as it may seem, he is lured there (like *Assemblage*) by his search for the new.

The question of the new has been raised frequently in the last few of years, especially in the United States, where it always seems to be on the agenda. But more often than not, this interest in the new is a complicated and often contradictory affair. The 1988 MoMA Deconstructivist Exhibition, for example, gave the world of architecture a new, 'avant-garde' style, while its theoretical underpinnings mitigated precisely against style, and against the new. As Mark Wigley, associate curator of the exhibition, wrote in the *Deconstructivist Architecture* catalogue:

> Even though it threatens this most fundamental property of architectural objects, deconstructivist architecture does not constitute an avant-garde. It is not a rhetoric of the new, Rather, it exposes the unfamiliar hidden within the traditional. It is the shock of the old.[5]

With the arrival of such news, many of those interested in little more than 'the new' moved on to other theoretical conceits, such as 'the fold', and on to other French theorists. Indeed, in the period between 1988 and 1994, there was growing and palpable disappointment with deconstruction, some of which was directed towards Derrida himself when, at the 1992 Anywhere conference in Yufuin, Japan, he refused to outline a project for the new, preferring instead to discuss deconstruction in terms of a formal structure he called 'faxitecture'. What this meant in practical terms was that Derrida did not offer the architects a clear way to convert deconstruction (as the theoretical protocol) into architectural form. Derrida's failure to offer a project of the new in fact became a kind of sour refrain mouthed especially by Jeffrey Kipnis during much of the conference.

Although it is impossible to know for sure, one can only imagine that Derrida's refusal (as well as the ascendance of Mark Wigley's more considered reading of Derrida as a Heideggerian) was one of the reasons for Kipnis' shift from deconstruction and its stated refusal of the new. Kipnis, you will remember, is a self-proclaimed Nietzschean. But, since this was the period in which Kipnis was becoming a designer and not merely a theorist (a larva to butterfly transformation that is virtually irresistible to architectural theorists), there are design implications as well. Writing in his now famous essay, 'Towards a New Architecture', collected in the *AD Folding in Architecture* publication, Kipnis decried what he called a general cultural disinclination towards the new: 'Briefly, it [this retreat from the new] manifests itself as a rationale which holds that the catalogue of possible forms (in every sense of the word form: institutional, social, political and aesthetic) is virtually complete and well-known.'[6] In an attempt to redress this situation, Kipnis offered a new set of design principles, all of which might be said to operate under the rubric of what he called intensive coherence, 'a coherence forged out of incongruity'. 'Intensive coherence,' he writes, 'implies that the properties of certain monolithic arrangements enable the architecture to enter into multiple and even contradictory relationships.'

Like Kipnis, Greg Lynn proposes to address the fluid and complex conditions of late 20th-century urban life by calling for architectural forms that are themselves more fluid and complex. Writing in the same issue of *AD*, Lynn criticises deconstruction's inability to produce new design techniques that might result in an architecture which is both internally coherent yet open to its exterior conditions. Instead, he suggests that deconstruction only gives us architectures which are incoherent and which have a conflicted, contradictory relationship with their contexts or exteriors. Deconstruction allows only static collaging of existent or rosterable architectural forms with existent contexts. Lynn wants an architecture, which, like those influenced by deconstruction, is heterogeneous, but he wants one that is also malleable, fluid and supple. Lynn thus looks outside architecture to the culinary arts, to Gilles Deleuze, René Thom, and other sources in order to develop new, folded, pliant design techniques which might result in architectural forms that are themselves pliant and fluid with respect to their external conditions.

Lynn has since developed more fluid and more temporally-based design techniques, including his impressive animation modellings enabled by Alias software, all of which, to cite his forthcoming book, seek to produce lifelike 'animate form'.[7] In essays such as 'Form and Field', first given as a lecture at the Anywise conference in Seoul, Korea, in 1995, Lynn argues that given the material and immaterial structural changes occurring today, architecture must become more animate – it must move! 'The classical models of pure, static, essentialized and timeless form and structure,' he says, 'are no longer adequate to describe the contemporary city and the activities it supports.' Lynn thus calls for motion-based design techniques, a new attention to 'shaping forces', and an anorganic vitalism, all of which are meant to engender a new relationship between a stable (as opposed to static) architecture as a producer of discrete form in productive tension with urbanism understood as a practice of shaping gradients within fields. Lynn argues that using animation videos to conceive the urban context as animate, as in-motion, allows us to understand the relationship between architecture and urbanism in a new way:

> Throughout history, movement in architecture has involved the arrest of dynamic forces as static forms through mapping. Thus urban fields and movements have been understood as the fixed lineaments upon which forms could be mapped. To work as an architect with urban forces in their nonformalized state it is necessary to design in an environment that is dynamic. Architects need to develop techniques like [D'Arcy] Thompson's model that relate gradient fields of influence with flexible yet discrete forms of organization. This means moving from an architecture based on the equilibrium of Cartesian static space to one designed within dynamic gradient space. Architecture will not literally move, but it must be conceptualized and modeled within an urban field understood as dynamic and characterized by forces rather than forms.[8]

Yes, absolutely, but one would want to ask why does architecture itself not move? Why is architecture itself not animate?

When asked this question by Jeffrey Kipnis at the 1995 Anywise conference, Lynn responded as follows:

Kipnis: Let me hold you accountable to the question, Greg. Because you stay at the level of dynamic animation, we could be fascinated by what we see, but because you do not resolve it as a fixed static object with materials, structure, and construction, at which point we see its real consequences, we're left fetishising the video rather than really understanding its design consequences. Is this true or not?

Lynn: I want to resist answering that question. In other situations in which I have shown material like this, the response has been, 'Well, are you saying architecture has to move in order for this to be an interesting design approach?' I would say no.

Kipnis: You say no, but you do not show us what happens when you take the motion away.[9]

If the urban context or field is a dynamic play of forces, as Lynn suggests, does this mean that architecture is no more than a static form that arrests those forces? Lynn states the opposite: that architecture should no longer be understood as static forms, but as stable forms which dynamically give order to an urban field. This is precisely what we see in his animations: architecture as a dynamic force shaping other dynamic forces. But when it becomes form, the audience asks, when it becomes architecture, does it remain dynamic? Lynn cannot answer: the implication is that when it is being designed it is animate, but not architecture; when it becomes architecture, however, when it becomes a form, it becomes static. Is this because for Lynn, as for Kipnis and *Assemblage*, architecture is only the object-form at the end of the process? If architecture is stable and not static, as Lynn insists it must be, and if it is temporally inflected, implying movement, why does his architecture not move? Why does it not flow like the urban context with which it presumably interacts? Why does the movement stop when it becomes form? Why does his architecture stop moving when it is no longer design technique and becomes architecture? The answer lies with Peter Eisenman.

Lynn's critique of static form in the above cited essay, and typology and deep structure in his Cardiff essay, is an implicit critique of Peter Eisenman, the unofficial dean of the American avant-garde, and Lynn's former employer and mentor. Lynn wants new forms which respond to the new, dynamic, fluid conditions of late 20th-century urban life; animate forms in particular. However, as we have seen, he is only able to offer animate techniques which produce, in the end, forms that seem no more animate than those he sets out to surpass. Eisenman, unlike Lynn, is not interested in new forms which might deal better with the new conditions of the late 20th century, but in dislocative forms which call into question what he calls the metaphysic of architecture. It is this activity which defines architecture for Eisenman. The essence of the act of architecture, he says, 'is the dislocation of an ever re-constituting metaphysic of architecture'. In his essay 'Misreading' he writes:

The history of architecture can be seen as the continual rereading, and misreading, of the metaphysic of architecture

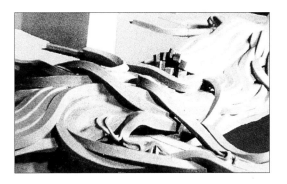

Topological architecture – FROM ABOVE: Philip Johnson, Gate House, New Canaan, Connecticut, 1995 – exterior and interior; Peter Eisenman, Staten Island Ferry Terminal, winning proposal, 1997; Greg Lynn, Stranded Sears Tower, model, 1992; Rem Koolhaas, Kunsthal Gallery, Rotterdam, The Netherlands

through successive dislocations, and the subsequent institutionalization of each dislocation, which thereby reconstitutes the metaphysic.[10]

Eisenman's architectural project is consistent with Derrida's philosophical project; both are simultaneously transgressive and conservative in their respective discourses; and both dialogic with those discourses in the very terms given them by the discourse. For Derrida this is the language of Heideggerian metaphysics, and for Eisenman, this is form. I say this only to note the connection between Eisenman's dislocation and Derrida's deconstruction, both of which differ fundamentally from the work of Gilles Deleuze, whom Lynn often cites.

For Eisenman, the new is not even desirable in itself, and that is because it often conceals beneath its newness this metaphysic of architecture. Eisenman's critique of modern architecture takes precisely this form: while it seemed new and different from the *beaux arts*, modern architecture's functionalism is consistent with humanist or anthropocentric architecture dating from the Renaissance. Modern architecture, despite its new, technologically derived forms, still operated within the metaphysics of humanism, and so while new, modernism was not dislocative.

This metaphysic of architecture is arranged around what Eisenman today calls an interiority, or by any other name an epistemology or ideology. Much of his own work, from the early essays and houses, to his most recent projects, has attempted to destabilise the interiority of functionalist humanism that dominated modernism, and that, in his opinion, persists today in even the most sophisticated architectures. Eisenman argues that architecture should never, as modernism did, place itself in the service of any exterior discourse, such as politics, or philosophy, but should instead articulate itself as an autonomous practice of form following form. Even when architecture turns to its exterior, as Eisenman did with Chomskian linguistics, psychoanalysis, deconstruction, folding, etc, it must always do so with the aim of dislocating and relocating the interiority of architecture itself, and that interiority for Eisenman is always form.

Eisenman thus always carries out his project of dislocating the metaphysic of architecture on the object itself, or rather one should say that the mark of this dislocative project is always registered as form. For Eisenman, great architecture – characterised by what he calls 'presentness' – dislocates by its form a previous form or type, forever transforming that type. He often cites his own Columbus Convention Center in Columbus, Ohio, as architecture which, while it might be new and interesting, is not dislocative. His Wexner Center, also in Columbus, Ohio, on the other hand, is a form which he argues calls into question the museum type itself, and as such is architecture that is dislocative and not simply new. Ultimately, Eisenman insists that architecture will continue to evolve only by turning inward: by focusing on its interiority; that being for him, in the last instance, form.

Lynn and Eisenman are literally pulling form in opposite directions. Lynn wants new forms which answer to new, exterior conditions, but he neglects the critical question raised by Eisenman about the interiority of architecture; about, in other words, what architecture is and does. Eisenman calls into question architecture's humanist interiority – architecture, that is, as a practice of housing and making safe. But he does this only in order to establish a new interiority, that of form generation. Eisenman wants to replace the humanist, modernist, form-follows-function interiority with a form-follows-form interiority. Lynn, on the other hand, wants to move architecture away from this interiority to its

exteriority, from static form – typologies, deep structures, etc – to stable form which interacts with the dynamics of its urban context. But he can do so only from within Eisenman's interiority of form; that is, he can only move to architecture's exterior, to something other than form, by way of form itself.

Thus, rather than questioning Eisenman's interiority of architecture, rather than questioning the status of architecture as a generator of form (as he does, for example with urbanism which he insists is an animate field of forces), Lynn accepts this interiority and takes form generation as far as it will go. He tries to make form animate, he tries to take form out to meet its urban exteriority, but in the end, he is only able to devise more and more animate techniques to design what are ultimately static forms. But if Lynn were to raise the question that Eisenman does, if he were to question architecture's interiority, he would then be able to move beyond Eisenman's interiority of form to a new consideration of architecture as a new kind of urbanism in-transit; something I have argued is at the centre of the work of a number of young Dutch architectural offices.

The real question not only for Lynn, but for this form-driven American avant-garde, is whether they will be able to discover a dislocative architecture that, rather than dislocating form or type, dislocates the form of architectural practice itself; that, in other words, calls into question the interiority of architecture as a practice of form production, opening it to the kind of expansion that has occurred in the Dutch context where the freshest practices focus on animate forms of practice, not on animate forms. Such a dislocation would necessarily take leave of the discourse of architectural interiority altogether and focus on architecture as a practice of fixity that manipulates or exploits movement in order to induce the production of new urban life. Architecture would then be able to become both a stabilising *and* an animating force in the metropolis without feeling compelled to make its forms move.

As Rem Koolhaas has observed in his distinction between Mies and Rietveld, there are practices which fix in order to open up avenues of freedom, and those that seem to offer an infinity of choice but which give no choice or freedom. Forms that 'look like' they are fluid with their urban contexts may in fact interdict, and forms which 'look like' they are interdictive may in fact be fluid with their urban contexts. If this were to be recognised, the question would no longer be 'what is the essence of architecture?', (form, light, image, etc) but 'what can architecture do' when it looks to its exterior, to the globalised metropolis?

This is a question that Eisenman, Lynn, Kipnis, *Assemblage*, and indeed the entire American avant-garde seem never to ask, and that is because they are always stopped at the border, stopped by form. Only such a dislocation can guarantee architecture continuous life in a world in which it seems to have lost its object, its mission and its way. Indeed, this is precisely what is at stake in Koolhaas' 'Bigness', in which the art of architecture must give way to a reduced, and interconnected set of practices that 'depend', as he says: on technologies, engineers, contractors, manufactures and currency markets. This is also what is at stake in the new practice of urbanism implied in 'What Ever Happened to Urbanism?', an approach and not a professional practice which takes up the problem of shaping the conditions under which new urban life can emerge and proliferate. Of course this is also what is at stake in Sanford Kwinter's 'new pastoralism', and Bernard Cache's insistence that architecture is the art of the frame, that it is the framing of the conditions under which life emerges.

Ultimately, architecture will have to develop a dynamism that matches that of the globalised metropolis. In order to do so, it must become, among other things, an animate form of form shaping, a practice of creating forms which themselves may not be animate, but which induce or create the conditions under which new urban life will emerge. The real implications of architectural ecologism, of which the work of Greg Lynn is just one example, will only be understood when we begin to think more clearly about how the practice of architecture can adapt to the turbulent conditions of late 20th-century life, how it can become something different, and yet remain the same, remain architecture. Perhaps *the practice of architecture* should become everything Lynn says about form and about technique: a pliant system, a blob, a semi-fluid/semi-solid practice, or even a body, as defined by Lynn in a recent text in which he again turns to the exteriority of architecture:

> For Margulis, a body is not an ordered whole but a provisional colony of previously discrete free-living entities that fuse together to live as a collective of organs able to reproduce and sustain themselves as a complex. These complexes can then become the organs of higher-order complexes through further linkages, exchanges, parasitisms, and codependencies. Instead of analyzing a body to find its essential structure, the insight resides in the functional and machinic behaviors of all the organs, in their ability to behave as an ensemble with the coherence and stability of a singular organism. The new concept of the organism resembles the definition of an ecosystem, which has no single identity but exhibits self-regulation and persistence nonetheless.[11]

Lynn cites this account of the body as a way to illustrate the new model of the body implied in his wonderful 'blob' architectural forms. But what if this model took him and us past those architectural forms, past the border of Eisenman's formalist interiority? If we were to understand architecture itself as a provisional colony of discrete practices, then urbanism might also be redefined as a dynamic body, corpus, or corporation made up of smaller bodies, or 'living companies', as Arie de Geus, past head of Scenario Planning at Royal Dutch Shell, says in his book of the same title.[12]

In *The Living Company*, an important new study of corporate life, De Geus develops the thesis that only those companies which learn can make themselves adaptable enough to survive in the turbulent commercial reality that exists today. Unlike 'economic companies', which close themselves off to this environment, preferring the guidance of shareholder profits and short-term gain, 'living companies' are open to their exteriors and are motivated not only by profit but by a desire to survive, to live on as companies. The 'living company' is thus defined not by its product, owners, profits, or even corporate ideology, but by its sensitivity to an ever-changing, fluid, commercial environment.

The Living Company, like the account of the body offered above by Greg Lynn and surprisingly like the body put forward in Gilles Deleuze's wonderful book *Spinoza: A Practical Philosophy*, is favourably disposed towards its chaotic exterior from which it gathers new information, or as De Geus says, from which it learns. As in Lynn's account of supple systems, this triggers sets of internal regulators which increase the order of the system, and make survival more likely. In De Geus' account, corporate learning occurs by way of scenario planning. Scenario planning attempts to project scenarios of possible futures that the company might find itself living; it does this in order to access and make visible virtual paths of company movement which are constructed from analysing the turbulent environment itself. Scenario planning is not predicative, however, not employed to reduce disorder, thus making the right path or plan obvious. Instead, scenario planning allows a company to increase order through learning, and as a result to enhance its own flexibility and adaptability to conditions over which it has no control.

To return more explicitly to Lynn's Cardiff text, 'The Renewed Novelty of Symmetry', the living company breaks symmetry and increases order as a way of enhancing its own survival, while the economic company, in a desperate attempt to find the right or correct plan, refuses to acknowledge its exterior. Now I do not want to push this analogy too far, but De Geus' book, *The Living Company*, might have something to offer architecture, something other than a new set of design techniques. In short, it might offer architecture 'a pass' across the border of form, and thus a ticket to a new life in the new metropolis. Nowhere is the need for such a pass more evident than in architecture's recent turn to ecologism and vitalism. Indeed, one can only hope that architecture will follow the path of the living company, corporation, body or practice. If, on the other hand, this new vitalism or ecologism, of which Greg Lynn's 'animate forms' are but one example, continues to follow the plan of the economic company, closed to what is 'out there', then it will profit only those CEOs and corporate board members for whom short-term profits made in-form-creation are the primary objective. If this occurs, it will only be a matter of time until Lynn and other members of the American avant-garde assume their places at the board room meeting tables of such companies. Perhaps they have already been seated.

This essay was first presented as a lecture at the Berlage Institute in Amsterdam, The Netherlands, on 28 October, 1997.

Notes

1 See Michael Speaks, 'Just There Modernism', in *Nine + One: Ten Young Dutch Architectural Offices*, NAi Publishers (Rotterdam), 1997, pp18-25.

2 Cited in the abridged version of the Jury Report, *Archis* 12, 1996, pp 8-9.

3 See 'Computer Animisms (Two Designs for the Cardiff Bay Opera House)', *Assemblage* 26, 1995, pp8-37.

4 Greg Lynn, 'The Renewed Novelty of Symmetry', *Assemblage* 26, p14.

5 *Deconstructivist Architecture*, Philip Johnson and Mark Wigley (eds), Museum of Modern Art (New York), 1988, p18.

6 See Jeffrey Kipnis, 'Towards a New Architecture', *Folding in Architecture*:

Architectural Design Profile 102, Academy Editions (London), 1993, p42.

7 See Greg Lynn, *Animate Form* , forthcoming from Princeton Architectural Press.

8 *Anywise*, Cynthia Davidson (ed), MIT Press (Cambridge, Mass), 1996, p 97.

9 Ibid, p112.

10 Peter Eisenman, 'Misreading', *Houses of Cards*, 1987

11 Greg Lynn, 'From Body to Blob', in *Anybody*, Cynthia Davidson (ed), MIT Press (Cambridge, Mass), 1997, p171.

12 Arie de Geus, *The Living Company: Habits for Survival in a Turbulent Business World*, Harvard Business School Press (Boston), 1997.

GARY GENOSKO
THE ACCELERATION OF TRANSVERSALITY IN THE MIDDLE

et us begin in the middle, despite years of advice about having a beginning, a middle and an end. According to Gilles Deleuze and Félix Guattari, rhizomes are all middle. The middle is a place where rhythms are laid down. Plateaus also have this in-betweenness about them. It is difficult 'to see things in the middle'.[1] In spite of this difficulty, Deleuze and Guattari advise their readers to look to the conjunction, and 'proceed from the middle'.[2] Bear the difficulty of the middle, they seem to be saying, because it is worth it. Spinoza, Deleuze showed, could be read by way of the middle. What makes the middle so difficult? After all, it is hard to live down popular conceptions of it: middlebrow, middling, neither here nor there, don't rock the boat. Similarly, it was hard for architects to live down the in-between of the Las Vegas strip described by Robert Venturi, Denise Scott Brown and Steven Izenour:[3] big spaces between buildings that were secondary to the signs before them; in other words, big spaces framed by big symbols in unenclosed properties comprehensible at high speeds. (I do not want to suggest with this example that Guattari was sympathetic to *Learning From Las Vegas*; on the contrary, he was highly critical of the conservative reterritorialisation of capitalistic subjectivity that was celebrated by such concepts as the 'decorated shed'.)[4] Still, the middle, Deleuze and Guattari specify, 'is where things pick up speed'. In the middle, transversality accelerates:

> Between things does not designate a localizable relation going from one thing to the other and back again, but a perpendicular direction, a transversal movement that sweeps one and the other away, a stream without beginning or end that undermines its banks and picks up speed in the middle.[5]

By contrast, Andy Warhol's philosophy went from a to b and back again, without sweeping either away; his philosophy was stuck between two points and not transversal at all. I want to jump in, right in the middle, in order to be part of what I am writing about, without passing from one bank to another (beginning-end). The reason that one is told to have a beginning-middle-end is that these are localisable, linear relations, precisely the kind kept in line by the dictatorship of linear narrative and the signifier. The middle is fundamentally transversal, as readers of *A Thousand Plateaus* may remember,[6] and a transversal line is deterritorialising; there are no more localisable points, in other words, to coordinate passages. It is hard to tell, as we learned from Las Vegas, where the property of a given hotel ended and the in-between began.

Deleuze and Guattari worked 'between the two'.[7] Not together, but between; they each had their own rhythms, which kept them out of step all for the better, looking to other people and concepts, whom/which they saw quite differently. Their points of encounter became proliferating lines, shoots, tentacles. Deleuze, in a letter to his Japanese translator, Kuniichi Uno, remarked that Guattari never stopped moving; his mobility, and multidimensionality, made him like the sea, while Deleuze admitted that he was more like a hill, in that he did not move much, except on the inside, and worked with one idea at a time.[8] During the writing of the *Anti-Oedipus* they rarely spoke to each other; rather, one spoke and the other listened. Guattari flashed like lightning, and Deleuze was the lightning conductor. The concepts with which they worked slowly acquired an autonomous existence; they never reached a consensus on their meaning (notably, body-without-organs): proliferation was never smothered by uniformity. A similar autonomy characterised their conversations, marked as they were by an increasing number of ellipses, especially during the writing of *A Thousand Plateaus*.

Guattari's speed; Deleuze's slowness – the middle is dynamic. Impersonal forces pass through it from all directions. It is a site of transformation and passage. It is the interface of resonances and, as Marshall McLuhan used to say about non-visual or uncentred tactile space: it is characterised by the 'resonant intervals' of interfaces on a 'wired planet'.[9] McLuhan insisted, however, that the resonant interval of such space must be understood in opposition to the idea of visual space as centred, connected and homogeneous. Interfaces are irreducible to connections for 'there are, in fact, no connections in the material universe. Albert Einstein, Werner Heisenberg, and Linus Pauling have baffled the old mechanical and visual culture of the 19th century by reminding scientists in general that the only physical bond in Nature is the resonating interval or "interface"'.[10] As the site of creative interfaces between Deleuze and Guattari, the middle kept them disconnected, a-centred; not two molar subjects collaborating together towards consensus, but interfacing and intersecting beyond themselves as authorities, authors, a philosopher, a militant analyst, each with their own expertise. Interfacing is not, then, a matter of meshing together smoothly. But neither is it a matter of discordant clanging and crunching full of tension. Rather than become hung up in our understanding of the middle by dwelling on our favourite pairing (whether it is Deleuze and Guattari, Laurel and Hardy, Jagger and Richards), I wish to reflect on the middle's *transversality*.

Brian Massumi defines 'transversality' as 'revolutionary side-stepping'.[11] I once described it as the transference become vehicular.[12] What is sidestepped is the analytic relation of analyst-analysand, the dual relation, for the sake of the groups in an institution. But transversality is not strictly speaking transference at the level of the institution; the former new concept replaces the latter through the non-exclusive distinction between two kinds of groups: the subjugated group and the subject-group. Guattari does not choose society over the individual, although he certainly criticises shrinks for segregating hospitalised patients from the social problems outside the institution. Guattari wrote: 'The social relation does not constitute a beyond of individual and familial problems, since we have, on the contrary, encountered it in every psycho-pathological manifestation . . .'[13] Conversely, it is not simply a matter of introducing social alienation into the institution by recuperation of the social signifier; however, Guattari rhetorically emphasised the importance of the social relation with reference to the most 'desocialised' psychotic syndromes, in the same manner as he underlined the importance of language by referring to the silence of the catatonic. Massumi clarified the matter succinctly when he wrote, with regard to the theory of the group, '. . . the individual *is* a group. The distinction . . . is not between a group subject and an individual subject, but between two kinds of group subjects, both of which exist on the so-called individual level *and* the societal level *at the same time and without foundation*.'[14]

Any investigation of transversality must begin with its relations to transferential phenomena in and between institutionalised groups. Transversality (in groups of people in psychiatric hospitals, in particular) is opposed to verticality, a flow chart showing a top down organisation (a pyramidal administration), and horizontality, understood simply as coping by fitting in to the best of one's ability in a given situation (given the dynamics in a particular ward).[15] Both 'pure verticality' and 'straightforward horizontality' are different kinds of impasses which transversality tries to overcome. Transversality cannot be achieved if these sorts of impasses are solved through an order being issued from on high by the hospital administration (through official directives) nor by neglecting the structural dimension of blindness at the level of the ward or among the nurses, interns, doctors, among whom, and sometimes in virtue of whom, non-structural initiatives may be allowed to take place.

In Guattari's early writings transversality is thought of in terms of a coefficient: a quantity theorised with the assistance of a therapeutic bestiary (horses, porcupines, flocks of birds, and moulting animals, not to mention the creatures of the psychoanalytic bestiary); and in visual terms – actually, in terms of a degree of blindness or the wearing of adjustable blinkers by the members of the various groups in the institution. The adjustment of such blinkers is the work of the analyst. Guattari suggested the following of transversality: it may be low or high; it may be opened or restricted; it may be latent or manifest; it is homogeneous, even though different intensities exist here and there in the institution; it is a property of groups, and it is always present to some degree, just as the transference, as Freud once thought, was present from the outset of the analysis, in the somewhat banal sense that anyone who can libidinally cathect onto another person is engaged in a transferential relation. But transference is an artifact of the treatment itself: the focusing of the patient's illness on the physician and its transformation into a newly minted transference neurosis. Similarly, one may say of transversality that it exists in some measure in groups, but that it is neither trapped in a dual relationship over which the analyst lords, nor is it simply widened to the group and institution.

Transversality is generally facilitated by the maximisation of communication between the different levels of organisation in the institution. But an important clarification is in order. At this point in his career Guattari was still working with the Freudian manifest-latent distinction. So, when he writes of the possibility of adjusting (that is, strengthening or weakening the coefficient of transversality) he immediately appeals to two different dimensions of communication: manifest and latent. Now, transversality is unconscious. What this means as a working principle is that the groups holding the real power (read latent) in the institution do not necessarily coincide with the groups who manifestly run the place (the hospital is really run by the patients, or the family is run by the

children). This being the case, the levels of transversality in the groups with the real power 'unconsciously determines the adjustment of the extensive possibilities of other levels of transversality'.[16] Guattari continues:

> The problem of the real relation of forces needs to be analyzed. Everyone knows that the law of the State is not made by the ministries. Similarly, in a psychiatric hospital it may happen that *de facto* power eludes the official representatives of the law only to be distributed among various sub-groups: departments, big shots or – why not? – patients' clubs, staff associations, etc.[17]

On the level of the expression of reformist sentiments it is desirable, Guattari suggests, that the caregivers themselves (the doctors and nurses) 'control the factors capable of modifying the atmosphere, the relationships, the real running of the institution'. But an analysis based upon transversality does not accept the simple declaration of reforms, for this still implies a vertical hierarchy. What is to be discovered are the groups holding the real power. Holding power is not a static matter to be revealed once and for all: 'the subject of the institution, the effective – that is to say unconscious – subject, is never given once and for all. It has to be flushed out . . .'[18]

All of this has a rather explicit Freudian ring to it: the introduction of transversality in the group is equivalent to Freud's introduction of 'a new class of psychical material', the latent dream thoughts; thus necessitating the investigation of the relation, through the processes of the dream work, between the manifest content of dreams and the latent dream thoughts. The meaning of a dream must be 'disentangled', just as the group holding the real power must be similarly 'flushed out'. Of course, Guattari's debts to Lacan were also substantial, and he read the group (well, at least its symptomology) as if it were structured like a language, in order to investigate its speech and, in some cases, speechlessness. For Guattari 'transversality is the locus [*le lieu*] of the unconscious subject of the group'.[19] This definition brings to mind Lacan's definitions of the unconscious and the Other as loci of the signifier, for instance, or the unconscious as the discourse of the Other; entailing that one cannot know precisely what the subject of the group is but only know it as a locus of relationships, a locus being defined in terms of relationships rather than entities.

I will not pursue in detail Guattari's definitions of the two kinds of group subjects: subjugated groups and subject-groups. Suffice to say that the distinction, which is non-absolute, is maintained by appeals to the difference between the ability to make a statement (subject-group) as opposed to having one's cause heard, but without verification of where or by whom it was heard. The subject-group's alienation has an internal source arising from its efforts to connect with other groups, thus exposing its members, risking their security, responding with collective paranoia and neurotic obsessions; whereas the subjugated group's alienation is thought to have an external source, from which it protects itself by withdrawing into itself and constructing richly paranoid protective formations, providing a kind of refuge and a distorted sense of security for its members. The manifest-latent distinction is employed to indicate that the unconscious desire of the group 'needs to be decoded through an interpretation of the diverse ruptures of meaning arising in the phenomenal order'.[20]

As I mentioned earlier, this sort of group analysis does not attempt to grasp the 'static truth' (a universal) of a particular range of symptoms. Indeed, the analytic goal of the modification of the different coefficients of transversality existing in and

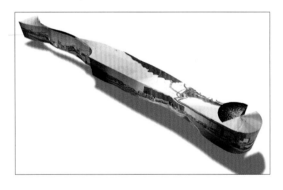

FROM ABOVE: 'Dialogue with the Knowbotic South': Antarctic research, 1996 – interactive visitor contacting a knowbot, outside view; view of knowbotic installation; Art + Com, Time Space architecture

among the groups in an institution cannot be said to be aligned with 'group engineering' or 'role adaptation', even though Guattari explicitly described how the 'strengthening of an existing level of transversality in an institution allows a new kind of dialogue to establish itself in the group', thus giving to a hitherto silent and withdrawn patient a 'collective mode of expression' for example. The patient's joining of a subject group, functioning in the manner of a 'pure signifying chain', allows them to 'reveal him/herself to him/herself beyond his/her imaginary and neurotic impasses';[21] whereas, if a neurotic or psychotic were to join a subjugated group, they would have their narcissism reinforced or find a place that would accommodate the silent exploration of their passions. And there is a certain freedom in this. Let us not label one group good and the other bad.

Elsewhere, I have noted that Guattari's two sorts of groups were modelled on Sartre's distinction between serial being and the group in fusion.[22] However, any reader of Guattari's essay on transversality can see that he very early on introduced a passage from Freud's late essay 'Anxiety and the Instinctual Life' (written in 1933 and published in 1965),[23] in which the distinction between anxiety produced by an internal as opposed to an external danger must have had some bearing on his reading of the sources of alienation in the two kinds of group subjects. More importantly, Freud maintained that there are determinants of anxiety appropriate to every developmental phase (ie, castration in the phallic phase), but that these are never completely dropped. Guattari seized upon castration – which Freud went to some length to justify as a real, external danger – as a key to social relations in advanced capitalist and socialist bureaucratic societies: there is no end to its threat, under various guises. Guattari considered castration to be a '*supplementary term* in the situational triangulation of the Oedipus complex, so that we will never finish with this threat which will permanently reactivate what Freud called "an unconscious need for punishment"'.[24] Understood as a 'social reality', this need for punishment will be blindly repeated. Its basis is an 'irrational morality', Guattari specified, since it cannot be articulated as an 'ethical legality': irrational to be sure, and a 'danger' belonging to the signifying logic of contemporary society. The threat of punishment plays, then, a regulatory role: it is blind but socially effective.

If the castration complex is never resolved satisfactorily and the need for punishment is repeated endlessly, it follows that the super ego's growth will be stunted and the ego will be sacrificed on the alter – not of the father – but on the mystifications of great leaders who are at once fathers-kings-gods, and whose abilities to actually intervene in 'the signifying machine of the economic system' were not very great, even though they were 'collectively pseudo-phallicised' by voters or the party, depending on the political system at issue. Presumably, it is the castration complex that compels the little boy to give up his Oedipal attachments to mommy and daddy; with little girls, things are quite different because the threat of castration does nothing to destroy the Oedipus complex. Consequently, Freud mused, the formation of the little girl's super ego is impaired. The point of this diversion into Freud's formulations is to show that Guattari believed that the analyst must attend very carefully to the 'goal of modifying the data "received" by the super ego, transmuting such data in a sort of new "initiatic" reception, clearing from its path the blind social demand of a certain castrative procedure to the exclusion of all else'.[25] The modification of the super ego of a patient in an institutional context would give a radically peripatetic character to psychoanalysis. It would get shrinks out from behind the couch and out of their offices, not only into the hospitals, and on to the floors of the wards, but into the kitchens and grounds, and out into the sector; that is, into the community. What Guattari envisaged was a geo-psychiatry.[26]

'How can the head physician,' Guattari wondered, 'be convinced to accept and even solicit questions about his actions, without having him recoil before the panic fear of being torn to bits?'[27] The doctor's acceptance of this questioning, his/her 'assumption of the phantasm of breaking apart . . . plays an essential role in the setting up of a structure of transversality' and the modification of the data received by the super ego of the patients (and, indeed, of the doctor as well). This assumption puts the doctor into direct contact with the phantasms of the group, and enables the group to learn a new role, and to question and redefine old roles. It is through this process that the aforementioned 'initiatic' acceptance of new data by the super ego may be brought about, primarily by setting up ego ideals which directly affect what the super ego incorporates; castration does not evaporate but, instead, it is 'articulated with social demands different from those that the patients have previously known in their familial, professional and other relations'.[28] The castration complex can be modified according to local conditions.

This is precisely the role that Guattari sought to play in his work at La Borde through what was called 'la grille' – the scheduling of rotating tasks undertaken by medical and support staff, in concert with the founding and organisation of patients' clubs not bound by the vertical hierarchies of the institution. The goals of these activities were multiple, for not only was a transversal structure set up to enable a certain reciprocity to prevail between groups hitherto divided hierarchically, but to create an atmosphere in which hitherto repressed phantasies could come to light; not to mention that new encounters with different institutionally-based matters of expression (the head physician working in the kitchen, and the kitchen staff overseeing the rounds) were facilitated by the desegregation of roles, breaking the grip of routine and boredom with the opportunity for improvisation, innovation and experimentation. It should be said that none of this guaranteed warm, fuzzy group togetherness. Constant questioning is risky, for where there are reassurances there are also obsessive defence mechanisms. It is not clear, by the end of Guattari's 'Transversality' paper, that the castration complex can be resolved successfully, even in the absence of a dual analytical situation that Guattari likened to a master-slave dialectic.

It is not difficult to generalise Guattari's example of the transversalisation of the analyst's work. His approach to architectural practice is a case in point. Guattari shifted his focus from the architectural object to the architectural project. He foregrounded the ethico-political choices involved in architectural practice, and considered that 'the reinvention of architecture can no longer signify the revival of a style, a school, a theory with hegemonic authority but the reconstruction, under current conditions, of architectural enunciation and, in a sense, the craft of the architect'.[29] He wanted to ask no less a question than 'how should one practise architecture, today?' His goal was not, as he put it, to put the architect on the couch, but to transversalise the vertical and horizontal reference points (the phallic architect at the summit of the 'firm'; the dean of the architecture school, down to the users of a building, including perpendicular critical relations to the object etc), and rethink the relative weights given to all the actors/operators involved in an architectural enunciation.

Reflecting on his own experience in a variety of militant organisations (youth and party) in the 1950s in an important essay 'The Group and the Person', Guattari remarked that regardless of whether or not the groups actually had any real effect, the important thing was, rather, that 'certain types of action and concentration represented a break with habitual social processes and, above all, a rupture with the modes of communication and emotional demonstration inherited from the family.'[30] This rupture was critical in distinguishing between subject and what Guattari then called 'object' groups (corresponding to subjugated), and in addition presented 'a minimal possibility of taking hold of the desire of the group . . . and a possibility of escaping from the immutable determinisms whose models are furthered by the structure of the nuclear family, the organisation of labour in industrial societies (in terms of wages and hierarchies), the Army, the Church, the University'; in Freud's group psychology, one may recall, the Church and the Army served him as primary examples of complex, artificial groups with leaders which furthered his characterisation of the group by the libidinal ties between its members and with its leader(s), that is, horizontal and vertical relations.

Clearly, then, transversality was a key element of a militant practice borne of a rupture with inherited models of organisation. To transversalise the organisation of a given institution was a creative revolutionary act, and the subject group was able to internally generate and direct its projects, ensuring that organisation remained tied closely to it, while simultaneously avoiding the slide into bureaucratic sclerosis; diagramming the 'Leninist rupture' and the rise of the molar dictatorship of Stalin, for example, suggested that the most excessive repressive measures were required to equal and exceed the 'richest current of social expression history has known'.[31]

Militants are often condemned to the phantasms of subjugated groups which prevent them from exploring the 'real texture of an organisation'; they get hung up on the significations produced by leaders rather than producing their own signifiers and speaking in the name of the institutions they create adequate to the course of their actions (not a party and its lines for these are 'machines of repression producing anti-production, that is, signifiers which plug and prohibit the emergence of all subjective expressions of the group'). Similarly, even subject groups may become bewitched by their own phantasies, losing their sense of direction for a time; these phantasies are transitional, however, and correspond to changes inside the group, rather than those requiring the subordination of the group.[32] In *Anti-Oedipus* the discussion of this point emphasised the mutual imbrication of the groups while maintaining the distinction between real, non-hierarchical coefficients of transversality and symbolic structures of subjugation, using the language of opening and closing to thread the subject-subjugated distinction through the fabric of desiring-production.[33]

I would like to place Guattari's early elaboration of transversality in the context of the development of his thought by jumping ahead to his final published work, *Chaosmosis* (1992).[34] I need only remind the reader to keep in mind a series of modifications that have taken place in his relationship to psychoanalysis. Consider, then, Guattari's first essay in the book, 'On the production of subjectivity'. His transversalist conception of subjectivity escapes the individual-social distinction as well as the givenness or preformedness of the subject either as a person or individual; subjectivity is both collective and self-producing. *Chaosmosis* is full of refrains of Guattari's thought: his criticism of linguist

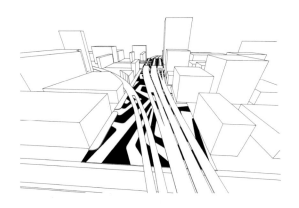

ABOVE AND CENTRE: Adriaan Geuze/West 8,
Park Teleport, Carrasco Square, Amsterdam, 1996
– perspective and mosaic of grass and asphalt;
BELOW: Ralph Applebaum, The Newseum, Arlington,
Virginia, 1997 – Video News Wall

semiology and structuralism in the name of an interest in a-signifying phenomena; a rejection of Freudian psychogenetic stages of development for the sake of a polyphonic conception of subjectivity of coexisting levels. These points are rather complex and I cannot fully explore them here, except to note that Guattari favoured what he referred to as 'pragmatic applications' of structuralism; one such manifestation was the psychoanalytic theory of partial objects, especially the Lacanian theory of the *objet a*, which Guattari read through Bakhtin, especially as it concerned the autonomisation of subjectivity in relation to aesthetic objects, the so-called 'partial enunciators'; these are the references by means of which subjectivity enunciates itself.[35] It is fair to say the only thing Guattari held on to from his Lacanian training was the theorisation of the partial object as the *objet petit a*. Transversality was worked through this Lacanian concept because it served, in Guattari's early paper 'The Transference', to critique the dual analysis (the mother-child relation is triangular to the extent that there is a third detachable, displaceable object at issue – hair or, even better, the mother's love.[36] Lacanian, Kleininan, and Winnicottian partial objects were all put into service, at one time or another by Guattari, to assist his construction of the institutional object, the mediating object beside the individual and group. But I will not pursue this concept here.

For our purposes, suffice to say that Guattari's shift into complex, hybrid, machinic semiotics derived from Louis Hjelmslev and John Peirce, and non-human domains, does not leave much of 'structuralist reductionism' in his thought. But the partial object survived and was generalised into an ethico-aesthetic theory of the subjectivation that escaped the shackles of personological and familial models. Partial subjectivation became a key part of a transversalist conception of the relation between, to adopt the language of Hjelmslevian glossematics as Guattari understood it, expression and content planes; the transversal relation at the level of form is between the phonemic system and semantic unities. But this initial relation was still too linguistic for Guattari.

This struggle against linguistic imperialism was felt in many fields. Throughout the 1970s, for example, the semiotics of architecture was plagued by its dependency on linguistic models. One finds a particularly acute example in Donald Preziosi's architectonic analysis.[37] Preziosi's semiotics repeatedly underlines the marked difference between architectonic significance and linguistic meaning, without departing from the linguistic model (see his hierarchy of signs) and, in fact, without giving up an impressive dualistic overcoding of 'every distinctive feature of organisation'. Guattari then envisaged a critique of the formation of matter into semiotic substance such that substance would be shattered with the transversal relation between enunciative substances of a linguistic nature and non-semiotically formed matter; between, then, the linguistic and the machinic orders, whose relation would constitute machinic assemblages of enunciation. His guiding idea was to describe form-matter relations that skirted the category of substance, on both the planes of expression and content, and to christen these a-signfying semiotics, as a way out of glottocentric semiology, and a move towards the urging along and mapping of these creative subjectivations as they come into existence, embodying themselves in existential territories as they, to quote Guattari, 'extract complex forms from chaotic material'.[38] Guattari's schizoanalytic metamodelisation borrowed the categories of expression and content but opened and transversalised their relationship with the insertion of abstract machines at their points of articulation.

Guattari's interest in the production of subjectivity required a new model of the unconscious (actually a metamodelisation in the wake of such crises of modelisation affecting the relevancy of psychoanalysis, structuralism, marxism etc), beyond the work of both Freud and Lacan, loosened from 'tradition and invariancy'; that is, the objective truths of the psyche. Guattari became, then, a forward looking cartographer of the unconscious – centred on assemblages of subjectivation – rather than a backward-looking scientific interpreter of a restricted topography whose roads led back to childhood. Additionally, Guattari recalled his long-time break with the conscious-unconscious distinction and disavowal of the Oedipus and castration complexes.[39]

The analytic problematic shifts, then, from a backward-looking interpretation of the symptoms of pre-existing latent material to the forward-looking, pragmatic application of singularities towards the construction of new universes of reference for subjectivation. The heavy reliance on the castration complex that marked Guattari's early writings was subject, by the time of *Anti-Oedipus*, to a definitive critique.

With these points in mind let us consider what remains of transversality. I am not so much interested in its diverse adjectival deployments; rather, it seems to me that stripped of its psychoanalytic scaffolding – except for the modified theory of partial objects – and the institutional analytic framework in which it was originally conceived, the concept is radically opened to hitherto unimagined mutations and complexifications across all sorts of domains. It may be used descriptively, for instance, when applied to the solution Bernard Tschumi adopted in the hub of The Lerner Student Center at Columbia University. Sensing the transversality of an in-between space with one side a floor higher than the other, he used a system of half-floors with ramps to provide a continuous link to diverse student and public activities rather than divide the activities by full floors.[40] (The following proviso applies: all examples focused on architectural objects are, however, merely part of the larger requirement of a transversalisation of architectural practice as such.)

In other words, transversality still signifies militant, social creativity. Guattari was well aware of the risks of this kind of openness and the concept's progressive deterritorialisation from existing modelisations. He emphasised that transversality was not a given, an '"already there", but always to be conquered through a pragmatics of existence'.[41]

In his early works, transversality needed to be released and consolidated, but not towards a norm given in advance. Transversality was an adjustable, *real* coefficient, decentred, and non-hierarchical, and *Chaosmosis* put the accent on its in-betweenness: transversality as a 'bridge' is an idea that occurs several times; the concept retained its break with horizontal and vertical coordinates, its deterritorialising character, its social and political experimentality, and connection with production, especially the production of subjectivity, and the collective assemblages of enunciation. Transversality remained a line rather than a point. A line that picks up speed in the middle. Transversality can accelerate in the middle, but it better watch out for the 'speed[s] of subjugation':[42] the swiftness of reactionary clamp-downs and liquidations, and the shrink's or any professional's automatic turn to ready-made categories and conservative reterritorialisations.

The task today is, then, to find/create a middle through which transversality can accelerate.

Notes

1 Gilles Deleuze and Félix Guattari, *A Thousand Plateaus: Capitalism and Schizophrenia*, Brian Massumi (trans), University of Minnesota Press (Minnesota), 1987, p23.

2 Ibid, p25.

3 Robert Venturi, Denise Scott Brown, Steven Izenour, *Learning From Las Vegas*, The MIT Press (Cambridge, Mass), 1977.

4 Félix Guattari, *Cartographies Schizoanalytiques*, Galilée (Paris), 1989, p55.

5 Gilles Deleuze and Félix Guattari, *A Thousand Plateaus: Capitalism and Schizophrenia*, op cit, p25.

6 Ibid, p296.

7 Gilles Deleuze and Claire Parnet, *Dialogues*, Hugh Tomlinson and Barbara Habberjam (trans), The Athlone Press (London), 1987, p17ff.

8 Letter to Kuniichi Uno, 25 July 1984; handwritten manuscript.

9 See *Letters of Marshall McLuhan*, Matie Molinaro, Corinne McLuhan and William Toye (eds), Oxford University Press (Toronto), 1987, p504; and Marshall McLuhan, 'Man as the medium', in Sorel Etrog, *Images from the film Spiral*, Exile Editions (Toronto), 1987.

10 Marshall McLuhan and Barrington Nevitt, *Take Today: The Executive as Dropout*, Longman (Toronto), 1972, p86.

11 Brian Massumi, *A User's Guide to Capitalism and Schizophrenia: Deviations from Deleuze and Guattari*, The MIT Press (Cambridge, Mass), 1992, p106.

12 Gary Genosko, 'Introduction', *The Guattari Reader*, Basil Blackwell (Oxford), 1996, p15.

13 Félix Guattari, *Psychanalyse et transversalité: essais d'analyse institutionnelle*, Maspero (Paris), 1972, p73.

14 Brian Massumi, 'Deleuze and Guattari's Theories of the Group Subject, Through a Reading of Corneille's *Le Cid*', *Discours social/Social Discourse* 1/4, p425.

15 Félix Guattari, *Psychanalyse et transversalité: essais d'analyse institutionnelle*, op cit, pp78-9.

16 Ibid, p80.

17 Ibid, p81.

18 Ibid.

19 Ibid, p84.

20 Ibid, p76.

21 Ibid, p82.

22 Gary Genosko, 'Introduction', *The Guattari Reader*, Basil Blackwell (Oxford), 1996, p34; see also, Félix Guattari, 'La Borde: A Clinic Unlike Any Other', David L Sweet (trans), in *Chaosophy*, Semiotext(e) (New York), 1995, p191.

23 Sigmund Freud. 'Anxiety and Instinctual Life' (1933)', in *New Introductory Lectures on Psychoanalysis*, James Strachey (trans), WW Norton (London).

24 Félix Guattari, *Psychanalyse et transversalité: essais d'analyse institutionnelle*, op cit, p74.

25 Ibid, p75.

26 Gary Genosko, 'Introduction', *The Guattari Reader*, op cit, p11.

27 Félix Guattari, *Psychanalyse et transversalité: essais d'analyse institutionnelle*, op cit, p83.

28 Ibid.

29 Félix Guattari, *Cartographies Schizoanalytiques*, Galilée (Paris), 1989, p292ff.

30 Félix Guattari, *Psychanalyse et transversalité: essais d'analyse institutionnelle*, op cit, p156.

31 Ibid, p159.

32 Ibid, p167.

33 Gilles Deleuze and Félix Guattari, *Anti-Oedipus: Capitalism and Schizophrenia*, Robert Hurley, Mark Seem, Helen R Lane (trans), Viking (New York), 1977, pp348-49.

34 Félix Guattari, *Chaosmosis*, Paul Bains and Julian Pefanis (trans), Indiana University Press (Bloomington), 1992.

35 Ibid, p13.

36 Jacques Lacan, *Ecrits: A Selection*, Alan Sheridan (trans), WW Norton (New York), 1977, pp197-98.

37 Donald Preziosi, *The Semiotics of the Built Environment: An Introduction to Architectonic Analysis*, Indiana University Press (Bloomington), 1979.

38 Félix Guattari, *Chaosmosis*, op cit, p28.

39 Ibid, p12.

40 Bernard Tschumi, 'Deviance, The Normative and the In-Between', *Newsline* (Columbia University) 9/2, 1997, p5.

41 Félix Guattari, *Chaosmosis*, op cit, p125.

42 Gilles Deleuze and Félix Guattari, *Anti-Oedipus: Capitalism and Schizophrenia*, op cit, p349.

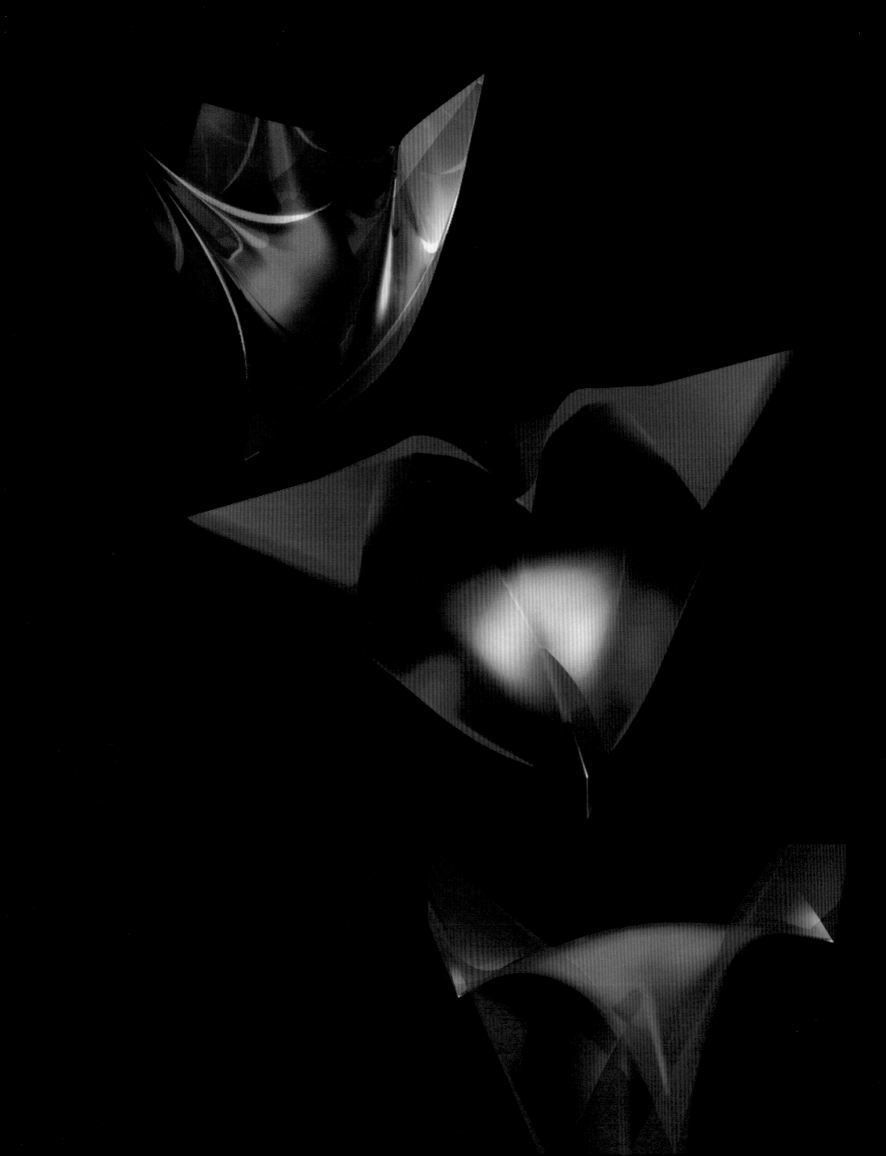

MARK BURRY

GAUDÍ, TERATOLOGY AND KINSHIP

A tavern waiter was discovered by Gaudí and became the Roman soldier for the Massacre of the Innocents on the Doorway of Hope. As it is related by Juan Matamala, 'When we asked him to pose, we found that he had six perfectly formed toes on each foot ... When he was obliged to put a pair of Roman sandals on him, my father wanted to hide one toe on each foot, but Gaudí interfered, exclaiming: "No, no! On the contrary! It is absolutely necessary to have them the way they are. It is an anomaly, just as it is an anomaly to kill children!"'[1]

The freak induces both pleasure and horror in ourselves as beings through a simultaneous expansion and contraction of our understanding of normality, a 'narcissistic delight at the shape of our own externality'.[2] Architects have been less inclined than philosophers to delve into teratology as a means to externalise their inner disquiet, preferring to seek other forces to sponsor the folding and pleating that accompanies much of contemporary building form-making. Antoni Gaudí is an exception. This essay considers the *real virtuality* of his later treatment of surfaces which are read as the formal boundaries, qualities that hover between the beautiful and the deformed.

Ideas of monstrosity inhabit more the domains of the natural and the supernatural than the unnatural.[3] In Western tradition, gothic masons made literal use of the supernatural in their sculpted reliefs and figures, many of which utilise the monstrous to represent the reprehensible. The nature of the carved stone surfaces projected by Gaudí includes a literal use of figurative biblical reference for the Sagrada Família Church and is entirely consistent with his medievalist intentions for this great unfinished work. The more abstract elements of this work demonstrate that he had an early understanding of aspects of our own post-modern abstraction: a belief that the organic life of architecture goes beyond the surfaces that appear to fix us from without and bind us within. However frozen worked inorganic or dead material might be, it is sufficient for other more volatile, more unstable worlds to be invoked from the grain of inert substances through their worked surfaces by implication if not by fact. Deeper than the superficial lie allegories we can unfold

by any means we might deem appropriate. In this respect, Gaudí's final project leaves more than can physically meet the eye, regardless of whether the project is finished or unfinished.

The Sagrada Família was established in mid-19th-century Barcelona to give a greater voice to the Holy Family during times of profound change and increasing social dysfunction. The 'Cathedral for the Poor' is dedicated to and promotes Joseph the father as the paragon of moral virtue and patriarchal head of family unity. The building follows the Gothic model rigorously in both scope and layered meaning. Gaudí, however, moved beyond this in his use of allegorical reference, as evident in the small proportion of the whole actually built in his day and in the surviving large-scale gypsum plaster models bequeathed to his successors. Beneath, and removed from, the stone and gypsum surfaces are sufficient clues that he was well advanced in his thinking about the elusive intangibility of free form, an intangibility lost when any free-form architectural composition comes to being as a building. Prior to his death in 1926, he demonstrated a complexity that foreshadows contemporary post-computer interest in less compliant form making. During this time he introduced ideas of metamorphosis, morphogenesis and polymorphism to this work. I shall describe an example of morphogenesis and link it to an architectural teratology and the notion of 'evocative surface'.

D'Arcy Wentworth Thompson's description and analysis of growth and form[4] was becoming known at the same time that Gaudí completed his detailed design for the nave of the church. We have no evidence, however, of any direct influence on Gaudí. While his interpretation may have much in common with Thompson's science, Gaudí's work itself contains ingredients that step outside the former's analysis of growth and include the deeper and darker areas of mutation and monstrosity. Such deviancy is entirely consistent with the moral mysticism of the gothic that he had applied consistently to the church during the 43 years of the design's development. In going beyond the superficial to less stable and more transient realms, we can observe Gaudí both separating and drawing together the contrasting ideas of kinship and excess as fundamental aspects of our human condition.

ABOVE: The Sagrada Família Church: OPPOSITE AND OVERLEAF RIGHT: Selection of frames from animations describing the deviant morphogenetic teratoids produced from alpha-n *to* beta+n *sequences*

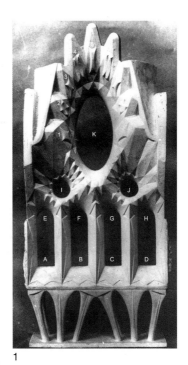

1

2

Fig 1. 1:10 gypsum plaster model of the Sagrada Família Church central nave window made by Antoni Gaudí between 1920 and 1926.
Fig 2. Detail of window: fourth order curves delineate the intersection of two adjacent hyperboloids of revolution; an example is shown here as d^1-d^2

Gaudí applied an expressive fluidity to all levels of the work for the Sagrada Família, initially constrained by Gothic Revival rigour as the building was commenced (by others). This fluidity is seen in the composition of the final design and the surface treatment of the design and sculpture, discussed here in that order.

It has long been recognised that Gaudí employed second order geometry for the entire composition of the nave.[5] Their relevance at a practical level was alluded to by Collins[6] but not unravelled fully until the 1990s.[7] The fundamental characteristic for second order geometry is the way non-coplanar straight lines can variously describe warped surfaces with a pragmatism that is masked by the apparently free-form composition. The principal practical advantage is the way each of these surfaces can be fragmented into individual components which, when combined, will form a seamless whole. If we take Gaudí's apartment building La Pedrera (c1906-12) as an example of the opposite position, free-form rather than ruled surfaces (note the semantic difference between *free* and *ruled*), we can see an important paradigmatic shift in Gaudí's surface modulation. La Pedrera required the masonry to be modelled in gypsum plaster at 1:1 in the basement on site, and for each piece to be carved at ground level, lifted to a position next to its neighbours, scribed and lowered back to the ground for refinement (a number of times). In contrast, ruled surfaces offer entirely different possibilities. Constituent elements can be carved once and carved well in isolation and without reference to their companions as the mason has to do little more than carve a series of straight lines between corresponding points marked on templates shared by adjacent pieces.

Gaudí had many reasons for this choice of ruled surfaces other than as an aid to building description. At an aesthetic level he is alleged to have made this selection in order to modify the play of light within the church and provide acoustic attenuation; these are noted as being his primary concerns.[8] But it is also reasonable to propose that the nine mathematical variables that determine the spatial characteristics of each surface give a fluency of assembly that no other three-dimensional compositional strategy can offer. Specifically, a hyperboloid of revolution of one sheet is defined by three Cartesian co-ordinates of location, three axes of rotation, two constants a and b defining the shape in plan and a third c that gives a slope to make a three-dimensional surface. A sphere has only four variables – three Cartesian co-ordinates of location and a radius; a cylinder has seven. We can assess these ruled-surface figures as having the characteristics and nuances of a family group in ways that the sphere and cylinder do

not; an infinite range of qualities, some subtle, some extreme, some good, some bad.

The family grouping is crucial in order to appreciate the sophistication with which Gaudí operated. A sphere enjoys no relationship to a cylinder other than both forms being grouped as 'primitives' or 'Phileban'. One sphere differs from another only in size. In contrast, the hyperboloid can be anything between a cylinder and two opposed cones with the aperture varying between a circle (let's say an ellipse with coincident foci for consistency) to a barely discernible slit. Beyond the unitary, each surface can relate to other family members with an astonishingly subtle bonding that only the mathematics of the resultant fourth order curves of intersection between contiguous surfaces reveal. Fig 1 shows the composition of the exterior of the central nave window which measures 7.5 metres wide by approximately 18 metres in height. Surfaces marked *A-K* are all elliptical hyperboloids of revolution. The decorative faceting is derived from the geometry as combinations of triangular planes bounded by selected intersecting *generatrices*, the lines that form the surfaces. The line d^1-d^2 shown superimposed on Gaudí's original model [fig 2] is an example of a fourth order curve of intersection.

The kinship of these geometrical forms goes further than the variables that tie each to the same species. Fig 3 shows the production of the applied decoration, which, at first glance appears to be arbitrarily based on the geometry but is actually a consequence of the composition. Equally, the emblems or motifs [fig 4] appear to be arbitrary but are neither whimsical nor entirely free from geometrical constraint. Each emblem might seem to be uniquely fashioned. In fact they are a single species with two genders: an *alpha* and a *beta*. Referring to fig 1, those marked *1, 2, 3, 4* and *5* are more specifically identified as *alpha-1, beta-1, alpha-2* etc. Not only can *alpha-2* and *alpha-3* be shown to be genetic variants of *alpha-1*, *alpha* and *beta* are morphogenetic variants of each other. As a group they share kinship. The proof is in the simple coding of an algorithm used to transform one to the other.

'Organic' architecture might be one of our more problematic misnomers. Buildings in their static condition are anything but organic, free form no longer free but fixed in the translation to built building. Too often, *organic* means that the built free form may do little more than bear characteristics attributable to natural form. One can speculate on the degree of frustration Gaudí might have felt in freezing life as immutable building fabric; certainly the stiffness of the sculpture (but not the setting) of the Nativity Facade is in contrast with other work of his mid-career. Our consideration of the relationship

3

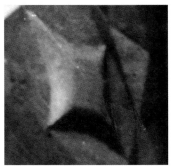

4

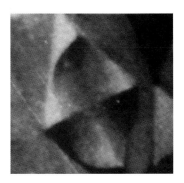

5

Fig 3. Detail of the decorative treatment, Sagrada Família Church lateral nave window. The decoration is entirely a consequence of the geometry, requiring in this case the excision of material (marked as a) and the addition (marked as b).
Fig 4. Detail of the decorative treatment, central nave window – the positions of alpha-1, beta-1, alpha-2, beta-2 *and* alpha-3 *are shown respectively as 1-5 in figure 6.* *Fig 5.* Sagrada Família Church Rosary Portal: 'temptation to violence'.

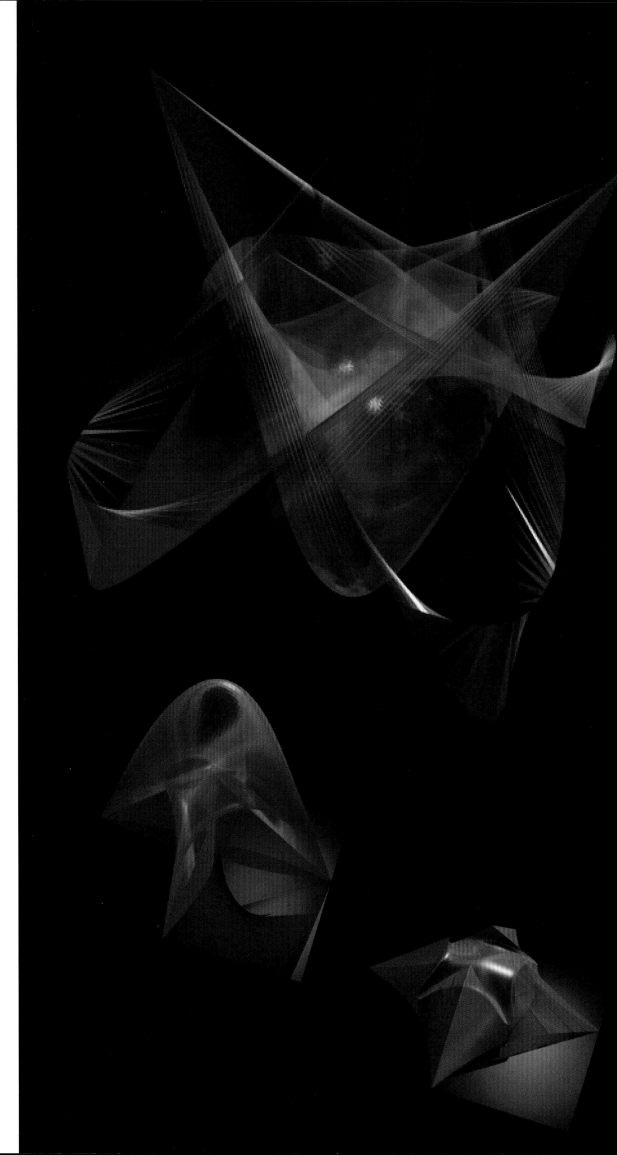

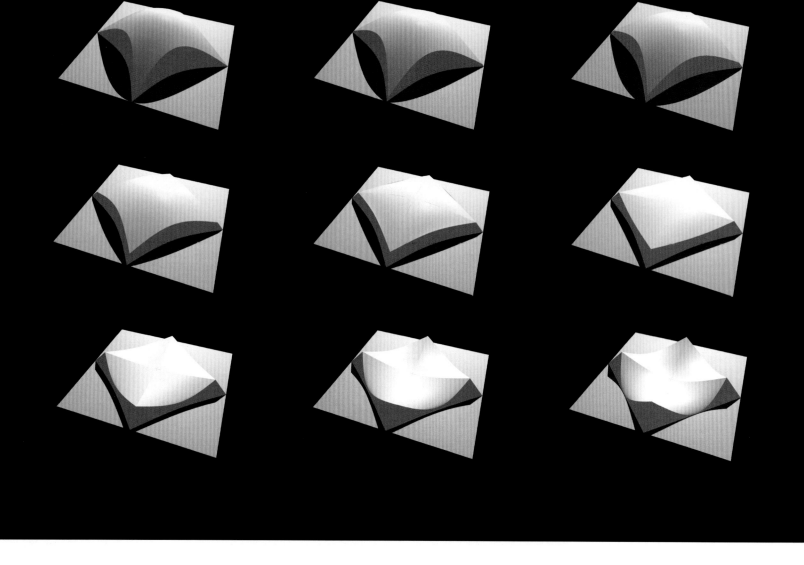

between *alpha* and *beta* is more easily explained through a fourth dimension: movement. The series of nine images [fig 6] shows a selection of frames animating the transition between the two opposites, *alpha* and *beta*. Note the neutering of the hermaphroditic dome boundary mid-morph: an *alpha-beta* hybrid.

Our speculation on the organic nature of architectural composition can go deeper into the hypersurface gene pool, the virtual rather than the real, beyond that which Gaudí has delimited through his models. In the case of this architecture, there are implications of being truly organic, attendant on our going further than the immediate and tightly-controlled constraints that give *alpha* and *beta* such poise and stasis, a reduction that is simply a constraint borne from actual construction.[9] What if we engineered a route from *proto-alpha* to *retro-beta*? By doing no more than altering two numerical parameters in the algorithm which produced the series of nine images in fig 6, the *growth extender* and the *age accelerator*, extraordinary consequences occur: a vigorous bolting growth spurt and a premature decrepitude going beyond the dignity of normal aging, or, in this case, that which is constructed. Fig 7

Fig 6. Selection of nine frames from an animation showing the transition from alpha *to* beta.

shows nine frames from the animated morphogenesis from *alpha-n* to *beta+n*.

We have considered here the family relationship between the nave surfaces and the elements bounded by their geometry. My morphogenetic and progeric reading may seem to move beyond any conscious creative thinking by Gaudí. As a personal reading it can, however, be complemented by consideration of his more figurative sculpture of the same period. The cloister, for instance, has an entrance arch that springs from two sculpted scenes on opposite sides. Both tell stories of corruption – one depicts the plight of a young woman tempted into prostitution, the other a man to violence. In the former, a perverted mermaid offers a bag of gold to the innocent. The companion scene shows a salamander with a meta-human head (as has the 'mermaid'), offering an exaggerated bomb to the anarchist recruit [fig 5]. Of interest is the extraordinary distortion of the human features to both creatures. It would almost seem that Gaudí has deliberately stopped the morphogenetic hybridisation of the human element before the process had fully developed. This suspended animation is an even more suggestive portrayal of the dance between good and evil,

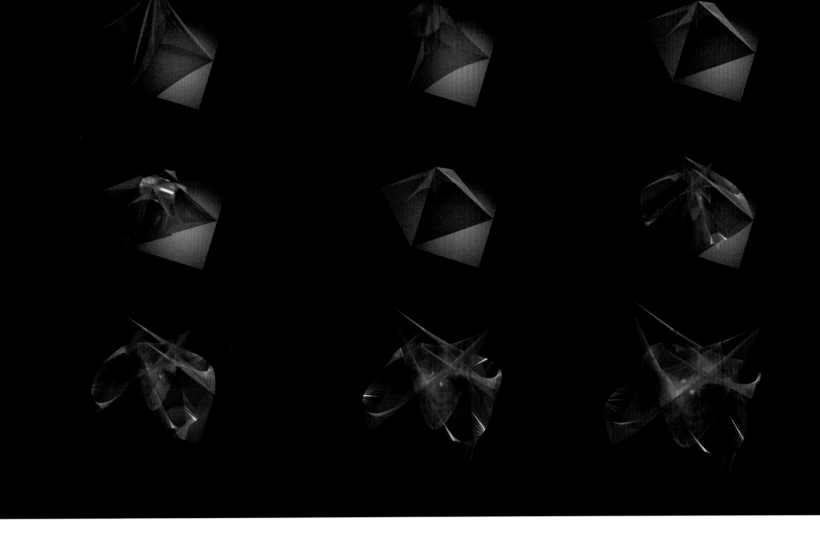

the freakish and the sublime, than that depicted by the gargoyles and sculpted relief of the Sagrada Família's gothic antecedents.

Whatever Gaudí's formal intentions, his surface composition for the nave was never realised in his time at any scale greater than 1:10, and never written about by himself. He nevertheless conceived and exploited a compositional geometry with rare grace. The animation or life implicit within the geometry is necessarily suspended as carved material, a static representation of kinship, variety and perfection. Yet the same surfaces provide all the clues and threats of violation and corruption through their concealed revelation of such potential. Read in this way, they are utterly indicative of humankind's striving for the ideal while one eye is kept on the monstrous, an ineffable benchmark and tally of extremes. The implied perfection is only skin deep. Closer reading provides the stimulation to extrapolate new ways to release the music and hear different architectural cadences to those with which we are more familiar.

With thanks to G Dunlop, G More and N Stephenson for their assistance in rendering the models.

Notes

1 R Descharnes, C Prévost, *Gaudí the Visionary*, Bracken Books (London), 1971.

2 E Grosz, *Freaks*, Social Semiotics, vol I, no 2, University of Sydney (Sydney), 1991, pp22-36. 'Our fascination with the monstrous human is testimony to our own tenuous hold on the image of perfection; the freak confirms us as bounded, belonging, a 'proper' social category . . .'

3 M Dorrian, 'Monstrosity Today', *Artifice* 5, The Bartlett, UCL (London), 1996. Dorrian includes images by Andres Serrano and Orlan in his piece all of which are unnatural images or juxtapositions. They are not examples of natural or supernatural monstrosity.

4 D'A W Thompson, *On Growth and Form*, Cambridge University Press (Cambridge), 1917.

5 I Puig i Boada, *The Church of the Sagrada Família* Ediciones de Nuevo Arte Thor (Barcelona), first edn, 1929, rep 1988.

6 G R Collins, 'Antonio Gaudí: Structure and Form' in *Perspecta 8: The Yale Architectural Journal*, Yale (New Haven), 1963, pp63-90.

7 M Burry, *Expiatory Church of the Sagrada Família, Antoni Gaudí*, Architecture in Detail series, Phaidon Press (London), 1993. Also, J Gomez, J Coll, JC Melero, MC Burry, *La Sagrada Família de Gaudí al Cad*, Edicions UPC (Barcelona), 1996.

8 The aesthetic qualities only were reported prior to the first actual building using Gaudí's second order geometry during the 1980s and not the practical advantages.

9 The fluidity of purpose is extrapolated from the built beyond that frozen into stone.

Fig 7. Selection of nine frames from animations describing the deviant morphogenetic teratoids produced from alpha-n *to* beta+n *sequences*

REISER + UMEMOTO
YOKOHAMA PORT TERMINAL

The proposal for this project (1996) was formulated in response to what was perceived as the inherent dichotomy between global systems of transport and exchange and the condition of the specific sites at which the systems intersect. Such conditions are exemplified by the port of Yokohama and specifically encoded within the programme of the port terminal proper.

In recognition of this liminal condition, the design sought to encompass the general functional imperatives of the cruise terminal (as a smoothly functioning link between land and water transport) and the specific civic possibilities suggested by the pier configuration itself.

In response, the structure was conceived as an incomplete or partial building – partial, both conceptually and formally, acknowledging that such programmes frame thresholds in two distinct yet overlapping continuums: in the cycle of embarkation and disembarkation of the cruise terminal; and at the civic level as a place of rest and recreation in the course of an excursion. Consequently, completion, both physically and virtually, is effected only periodically: in the linkage of terminal to cruise ship or in the closure of the completed urban event.

The proposed terminal is a shed building measuring 412 metres in length

and composed of 27 three-hinged, steel trussed arches of 42.5 metres average span, which are placed at 16-metre intervals. The arches are joined longitudinally by trussed members of conventional configuration, and purlins carrying either metal cladding or the extensive glazing envisioned for the project.

The steel shed structure springs from hinges placed at the surface of the main level. The hinges are carried on concrete piers extending from the basement parking level through the apron to the surface of the main level. Horizontal thrust from the arches is counteracted by tension rods connecting opposing arch

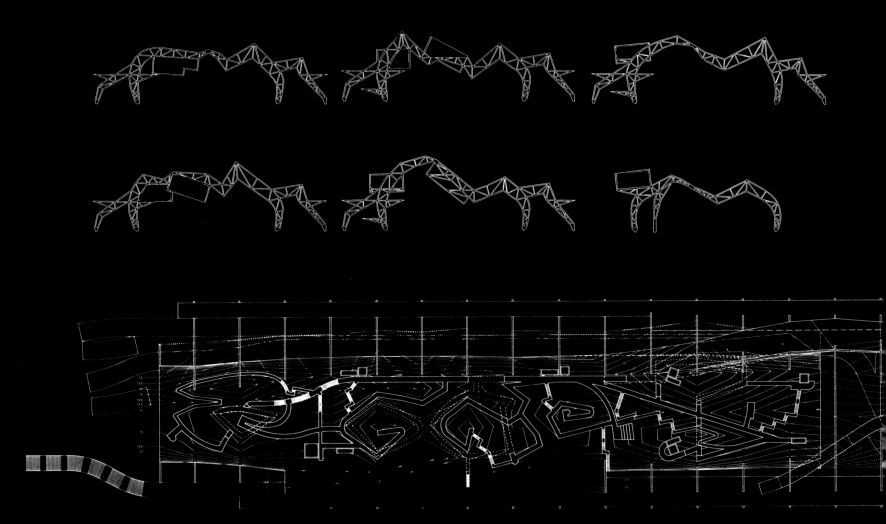

hinges. These tension rods also serve as partial support for the main-floor slab.

Although this large shed is affiliated with 19th-century antecedents, it differs in the sense that while such types were characterised by a totalising conception employing uniform and repetitive structural units enclosing a single homogeneous space, this project engenders heterogeneity through selective perturbations and extensions of the structural frames.

The transformation yields a complex of spaces that smoothly incorporates the multiple terminal, civic and garden programmes within and below its span.

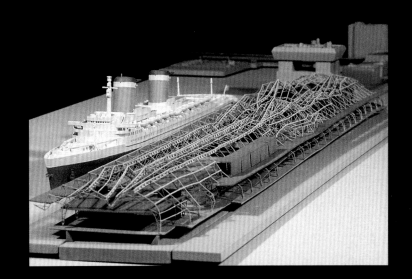

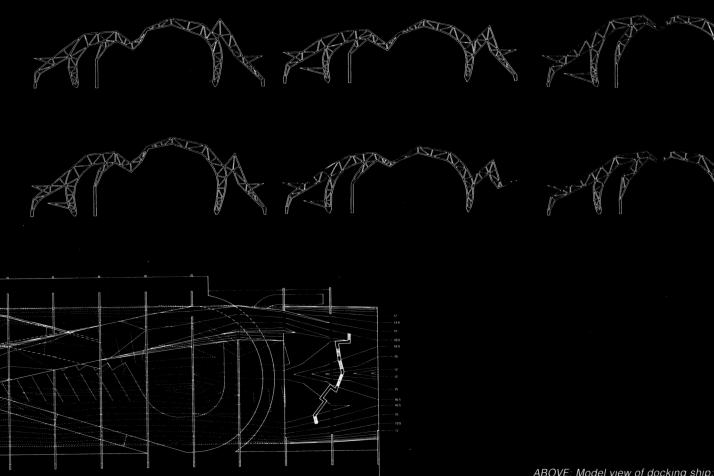

ABOVE: Model view of docking ship;
CENTRE: Structural frames;
BELOW: Roof plan

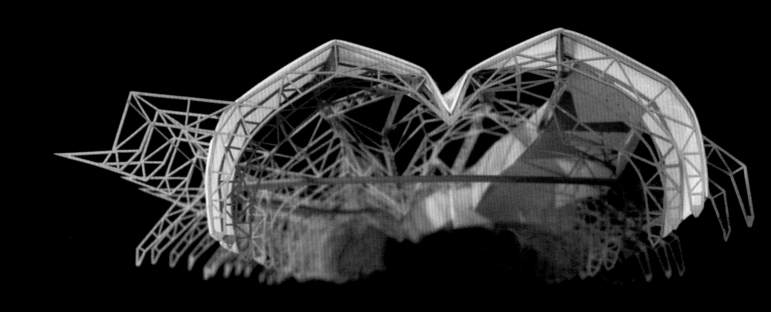

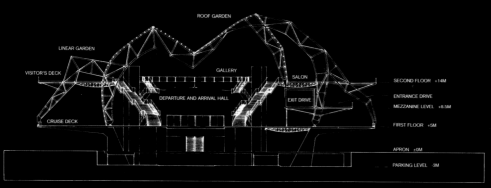

ROOF GARDEN

LINEAR GARDEN

VISITOR'S DECK

GALLERY

SALON

SECOND FLOOR +14M

ENTRANCE DRIVE

DEPARTURE AND ARRIVAL HALL

EXIT DRIVE

MEZZANINE LEVEL +8.5M

CRUISE DECK

FIRST FLOOR +5M

APRON ±0M

PARKING LEVEL -3M

SECTION AT DEPARTURE AND ARRIVAL HALL

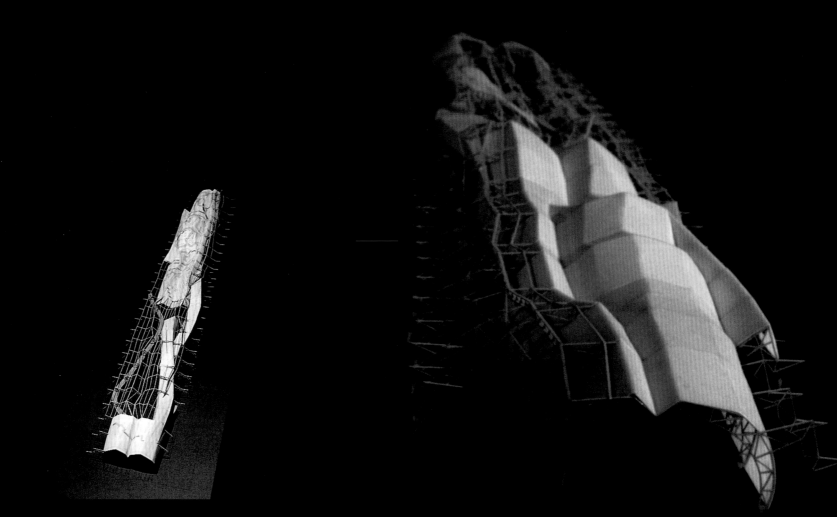

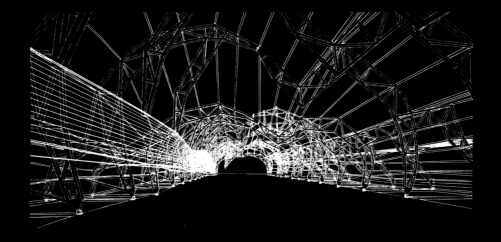

*OPPOSITE FROM ABOVE: End elevation of
pier tip; section of departure and arrival hall;
aerial view of model; view of roof;
FROM ABOVE: Perspective view; site model;
detail of roof programming*

LARS SPUYBROEK
MOTOR GEOMETRY

'There's this *thing*, this ghost-foot,' said one of Oliver Sacks' patients. 'Sometimes it hurts like hell. This is worst at night, or with the prosthesis off, or when I'm not doing anything. It goes away when I strap the prosthesis on and walk. I still feel the leg then, vividly, but it's a *good* phantom, different – it animates the prosthesis, and allows me to walk.'[1]

What is it that animates a mere mechanical extension? How is it that the body is so good at incorporating this lifeless component into its motor system that it recovers its former fluency and grace? The body does not care if the leg is made of flesh or of wood, as long as it fits; that is to say, it fits into the unconscious body model created by the different possible movements. Proprioception, the neurologists term it: the body's power of unconscious self-perception. Our legs are a 'comfortable fit' by their very nature, but only because the leg coincides exactly with the ghostly image invoked by the automatism of walking.

Once a leg is frozen in immobility, however, it very soon no longer 'fits'. Sacks reports one such instance: 'When, after a few weeks, the leg was freed from its prison of plaster, it had lost the power to make all kinds of movements that were formerly automatic and which now had to be learned all over again. She felt that her comprehension of these movements had gone. [. . .] If you stop making complex movements, if you don't practise them internally, they will be forgotten within a few weeks and become impossible.'[2] With practice and training, the movements of the prosthesis can become second nature, regardless of whether it is of flesh, of wood or – a little more complex – of metal, as in the case of a car. That is the secret of the animation principle: the body's inner phantom has an irrepressible tendency to expand, to integrate every sufficiently responsive prosthesis into its motor system, its repertoire of movements, and make it run smoothly. That is why a car is not an instrument or piece of equipment that you simply sit in, but something you merge with. Anyone who drives a lot will recognise the dreamlike sensation of gliding along the motorway or through traffic, barely conscious of one's actions. This does not mean that our cars turn us into mechanical Frankensteins but that the human body is capable of inspiriting the car and making its bodywork become the skin of the driver; this must be true, otherwise we would bump into everything. If we did not merge with the car, if we did not change our body into something 4 x 1.5 metres, it would not be possible to park the car, take a curve, or overtake others. Movements can only be fluent if the skin extends as far as possible over the prosthesis and into the surrounding space, so that every action takes place from within the body, which no longer does things consciously but relies totally on 'feeling'.

When this haptic sense of extension is taken seriously it means that everything starts inside the body, and from there on it just never stops. The body has no outer reference to direct its actions to, neither a horizon to relate to, nor any depth of vision to create a space for itself. It relates only to itself. There is no outside: there is no world in which my actions take place, the body forms itself by action, constantly organising and reorganising itself motorically and cognitively to keep 'in form'. According to Maturana and Varela: there is no structured information on the outside, it becomes information only by forming itself through my body, by transforming my body, which is called action . . .[3]

'Hey, we are lost!' Michael said to his guide. The guide gave him a withering glance and answered: 'We are not lost, the camp is lost!' In a flash Michael realized a very important aspect of what separated his vision of the world from that of his guide: for Michael, space was fixed, in which a free agent moved around like an actor on a stage, a vast space in which you could lose your way. The guide however saw space as something within, rather than outside the body, a fluid and changing medium in which one could never lose one's way when the only fixed point in the universe consisted of himself, and although he might be putting one foot in front of the other he never actually moved.[4]

This, of course, is a nomad's view of the world; the view of somebody on the move, because only by the prosthetic act of walking does the whole space become one's own skin. The tent nomads carry with them is part of that walking; it never interrupts space, as a house does. So every prosthesis is in the nature of a vehicle, something that adds movement to the body, that adds a new repertoire of action. Of course, the car changes the skin into an interface, able to change the exterior into the interior of the body itself. The openness of the world would make no sense if it were not absorbed by my body-car. The body simply creates a haptic field completely centred upon itself, in which every outer event becomes related to this bodily network of virtual movements, becoming actualised in form and action.

Where there is close vision, space is not visual, or rather the eye itself has a haptic, non-optical function: no line separates earth from sky, which are of the same substance, there is neither horizon nor background, nor perspective nor limit nor outline of form nor centre; there is no intermediary distance, or all distance is intermediary.[5]

In Tamás Waliczky's short film *The Garden* (1992), made with video manipulation and computer animation, we see a little girl running around a garden, extending her hands towards a dragonfly, sitting down under a big tree, climbing up the ladder of a slide, and then sliding down. We see all this and at the same time nothing like it. In fact, during the whole movie the little girl does not move at all, or rather, she moves her hands and feet, but her head never leaves the centre of the screen. We see the tree folding under her legs, we see the rungs of the ladder shrink and bulge under her feet, we see the slide deform under her body. Nothing moves, but everything changes shape. As the girl reaches her hand out to the dragonfly, we see the insect grow disproportionately large then shrink and disappear the moment she shifts her attention.

OPPOSITE: Nox Architects, interior of FreshH₂O eXPO (Fresh Water Pavilion), The Netherlands, 1997

The girl does not move around in a perspective world where things are between the eye and the horizon; rather, through her actions she is in perfect balance and stays fixed on the vertical axis: she has become the vertiginous horizon of things, the vanishing point of the world. Things become part of her body by topological deformation, not by perspective distortion. She has become the gravitational centre of a field, or better, a sphere of action – a motor field – her own planet . . . This is not perception but proprioception. Everything immediately becomes networked within the body, where the seen is the touched and the felt, where no distinction can be made between the near and the far, between the hand of manipulation and the sphere of the global.

An eye acts as if it were a hand; not as a receptive but as an active organ, and what is at hand is always nearby and close, without any sense of depth or perspective, and without background or horizon. So every action becomes prosthetic because it extends the feeling reach of the skin, and, vice versa, every prosthesis, and I mean every technological device, becomes an action, a vector-object, a twirl in the environmental geometry. Every change of muscle tone in the motor system has its topological effect, because outside and body are networked into one object with its own particular coherence, where seeing and walking and acting are interconnected in one (proprioceptive) feeling skin, without top or bottom but with an all around orientation; without the orthogonality of the vertical and gravitational axis of the body's posture in relation to frontal and horizontal perspective, but a three-dimensionality where images and actions relate to one and the same geometry, without any X, or without any Y, or without any Z.[6]

FreshH$_2$O eXPO, Zeeland, The Netherlands, 1994-97

Liquid architecture is not the mimesis of natural fluids in architecture.[7] First and foremost it is a liquidising of everything that has traditionally been crystalline and solid in architecture. It is the contamination of media. The liquid in architecture has earlier been associated with the easing back of architecture for human needs, of real time fulfilment. This soft and smart technology of desire can only end up with the body as a residue, where its first steps in cyberspace will probably be its last steps ever. But the desire for technology seems far greater and a far more destabilising force, since our need for the accidental exceeds our need for comfort.

FreshH$_2$O eXPO (as our design office NOX named the project),

generally known as the Fresh Water Pavilion, has been seized by the concept of the liquid. Not only its shape and use of materials but the interior environment tries to effect a prototypical merging of hardware, software and wetware. The design of this interactive installation was based on the metastable aggregation of architecture and information. The form is shaped by the fluid deformation of 14 ellipses spaced out over a length of more than 65 metres.

Imagine the curves connecting all the ellipses being torn apart, bent and twisted again by outside forces – the wind, dunes, ground water, the Well – while internal forces try to maintain the ellipses; that is, attempt to stay smooth. The basis of the geometry is the vector-based changing of splines linking the ellipses. In this way, line and force become connected. The spline with its control points and tangential handles in 3D modelling software derives from naval architecture where a curve was created by a wooden spline bend by the positioning of several weights at the 'control points'. Line is not separated from point, but every vertex is the basis of a vector. If one changes the position or direction of the vector, the others change in accordance with their mutual dependency. In this case, the line becomes an action, and not the trace of an action. H$_2$O eXPO is a bundle, a braid of splines. It derives its coherence from movement. In its soft network no distinction is made between form and deformation.

From the beginning, we wondered if we could design something that was completely in line with the law governing wheelchair accessibility (eg the steepness of ramps) while at the same time devise a prosthetic geometry, a geometry of wheels, a geometry of speed and imbalance? Not one part of the building is horizontal, no one slope stays within the same gradient. Conceptually, the building has not so much been 'placed on' the ground as 'dug out of' the ground. The essential instability is achieved through the concept of the ground as being 'all around'. The floor becomes hyperdimensional and tries to become a volume.

When dealing with a haptic, three-dimensional body – a body without the distinction between feet and eyes – the difference between floor and ceiling becomes irrelevant. With this kind of topological perception action is no longer ground-based, with your eyes transported blindly. Buildings are generally guided by this dichotomy of transport and vision, where the programmatic is on the floor and the formal is in the elevation. In this building, the information on the floor is blended with the deformation of the volume, to paraphrase Jeffrey Kipnis.

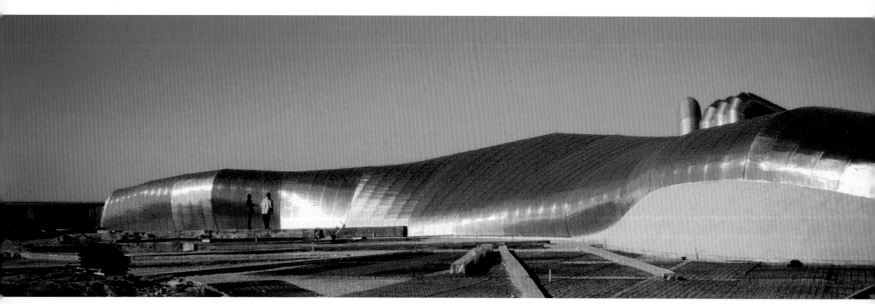

FreshH$_2$O eXPO (Fresh Water Pavilion), exterior views

In H_2O eXPO there is no horizon, no window looking out. There is no horizontality, no floor underlining the basis of perspective. This is, of course, the moment of dizziness, because walking and falling become confused; or, as the manual for 3D Studio MAX observes in the chapter on animation: walking and running are special cases of falling . . . This imbalance is the very basis of this building, and also the basis of every action, because not one position is without a vector. This building is not only for wheelchairs and skateboards, it is also for the wrong foot, the leg one happens to stand on . . . That is why, instead of a window, there is a well. The Well is another kind of horizon, more like a window to the centre of the earth: a hidden horizon, not horizontal, but vertical, on the axis of vertigo, of falling.

Where, then, is the point of action. Where is the source of the Well? Here, just like a surfer, the body is placed on a vector and obliged to react to that outer force, although it can change its direction or goal at any time. The architecture charges the body because its geometry is such that points become vectors. The source of the action in architecture that has become transported and moved – its geometry has become a prosthetic vehicle by contamination – is exactly in-between body and environment. This is not subject versus object, but an interactive blend. Part of the action is in the object, and when this is animated, the body is too.

The interactivity is not only in the geometry: the action moves through the material – not a form with a certain speed or on the move, but action in the form.[8] The design does not distinguish architecture and information as separate entities, nor as separate disciplines. The project is not restricted to materials such as concrete and steel, which were considered to be liquid, but utilises cloth and rubber, ice and mist, fluid water (taking over the action and wetting not only the building, but also the visitor), in addition to electronic media, interactive sound, light and projections. The material is not separated from the so-called immaterial. There is only substance and action.

The continuous surface of the interior is covered with different

sensing devices. Imagine walking or running up the central slope towards a wire-frame projection on the floor. In the course of this you activate a series of light sensors and step right into the projection, where you are covered in a grid of light. The waves begin to run through the mesh. Now you start to run with the waves, activating more sensors and creating more waves . . . The vertigo of the motor system is inextricably linked to sensory hallucination.

At the same time, the pulse of light going through the sp(L)ine – a line of numerous blue lamps – is speeded up by the crowd activating the light sensors. When you dare to step on a touch sensor, ripples suddenly shoot out from your feet: circular decaying waves in the wire-frame projection. Somebody else jumps on to the second sensor, a few metres away from you. Ripples then shoot out from their feet too, interfering with your ripples halfway. As you both begin to jump up and down you are pushing away the sound and activating the light running along the sp(L)ine: suddenly a high level of blue light splits in two and slowly fades away. Further on, a sphere is projected in wire-frame on a steep slope between handles that are gently operated by four people. Their action causes the sphere to deform in as many directions, while at the same time 'pulls the sound' from the Well. With their hardest pulling action, the light on the sp(L)ine is frozen in its last position.

Why still speak of the real and the virtual, the material and the immaterial? Here, these categories are not in opposition or in some metaphysical disagreement, but more in an electroliquid aggregation, enforcing each other, as in a two-part adhesive; constantly exposing its metastability to induce animation. Where is the sun in all this? Excluded and reflected by the outer skin of stainless steel, it is left behind in a museum.[9] The building is lit from the inside out, by the endogenous sun of the computer. This must be why the light is so blue: making hundreds of thousands of real-time calculations, shining on everybody, and rendering the action; the motor systems of the shadowless, spectral bodies coinciding exactly with the reality engine of the computers.

Notes

1 Oliver Sacks, *The Man Who Mistook his Wife for a Hat*, Picador (New York), 1986, p66.
2 Oliver Sacks, *A Leg to Stand On*, Picador (New York), 1991, Afterword, note 2.
3 H Maturana and F Varela, *The Tree of Knowledge*, Shambala, 1984, chapter 7.
4 Derrick de Kerckhove, *The Skin of Our Culture*, Somerville House Books, 1995, p29.
5 Gilles Deleuze and Félix Guattari, *A Thousand Plateaus*, The Athlone Press (London), 1988, p492.
6 Maurice Nio and Lars Spuybroek, 'X and Y and Z – a manual', *ARCHIS*, 11/1995.

7 Marcos Novak, 'Liquid Architecture', in *Cyberspace: First Steps*, Michael Benedikt (ed), MIT Press (Cambridge, Mass), 1993, p 225.
8 Maurice Nio and Lars Spuybroek, 'De Strategie van de Vorm', *de Architect*, 57, 11/1994.
9 Paul Virilio, 'The Museum of the Sun', in *TechnoMorphica*, V2 Organisation, 1997; *The Art of the Motor*, Minnesota, 1995; 'The Function of the Oblique', AA Publications (London), 1996; and *ARCH+* 124/125, p46.

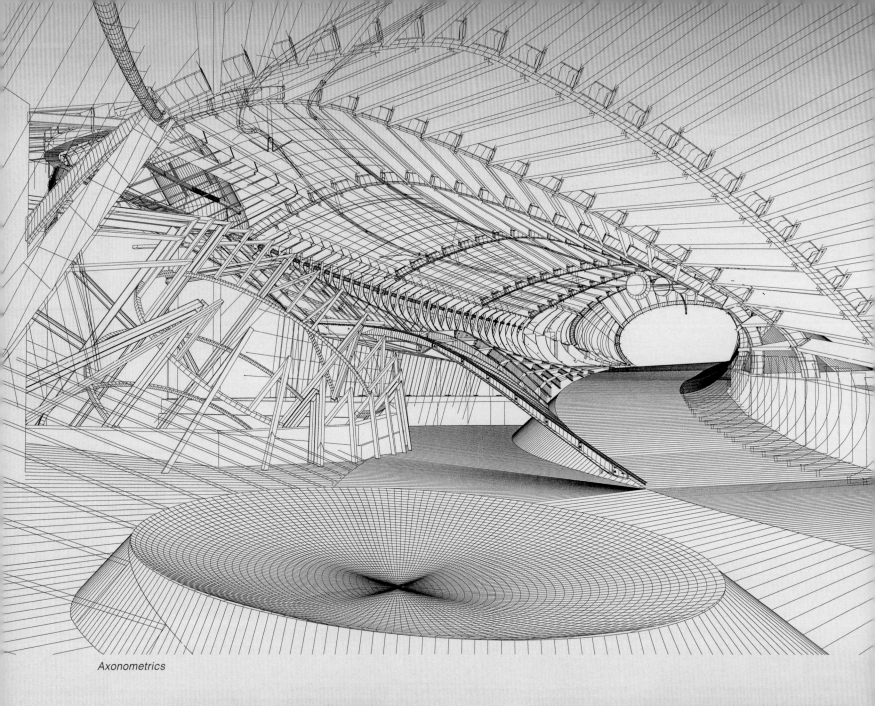

Axonometrics

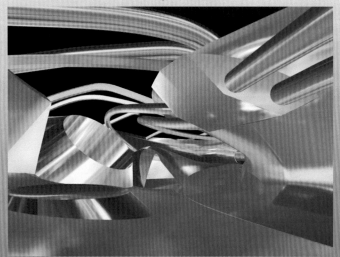

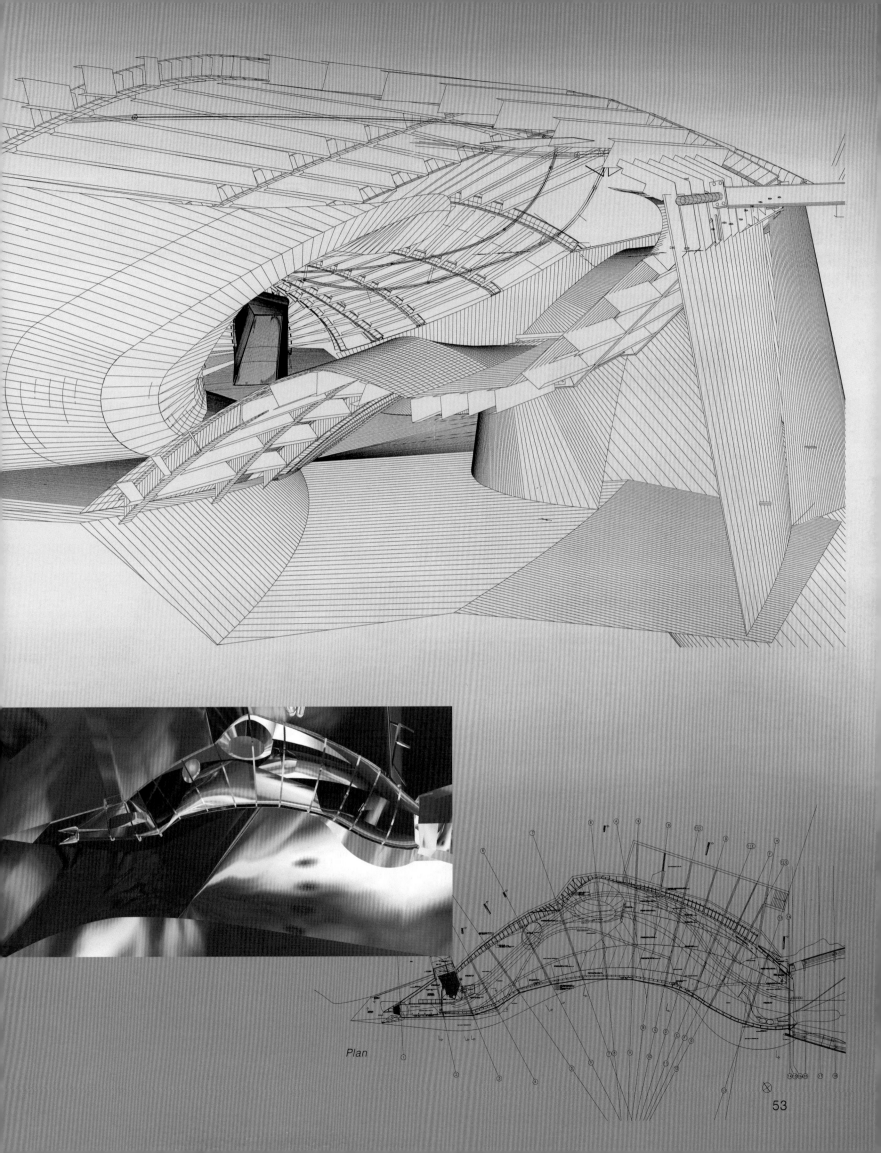

Plan

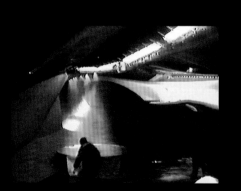

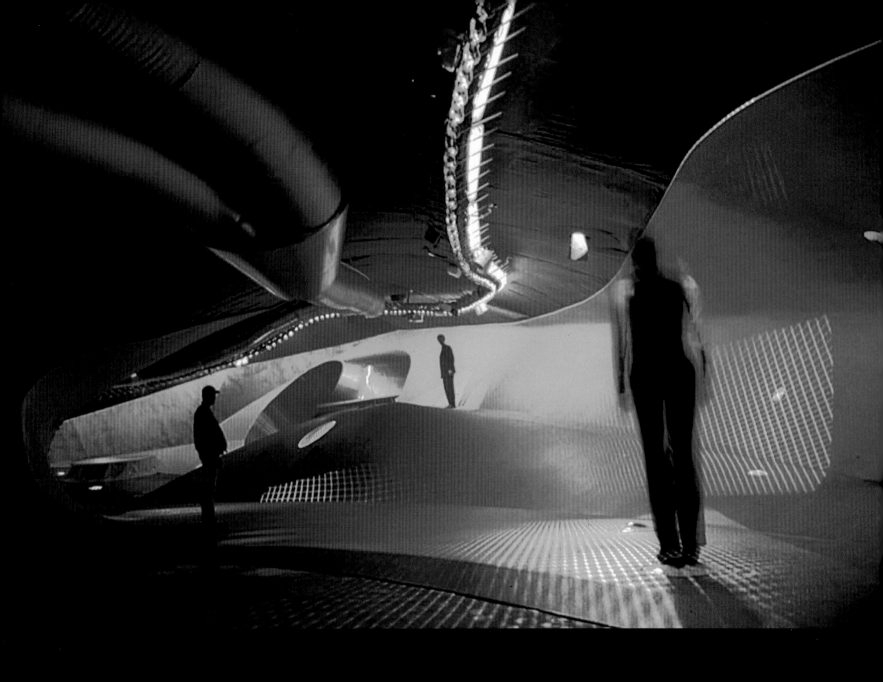

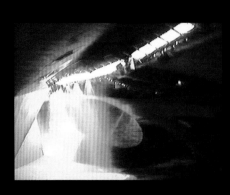
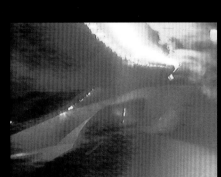

KAS OOSTERHUIS

SALT WATER LIVE
Behaviour of the Salt Water Pavilion

Real water

The Salt Water Pavilion is entered under a giant wave about 6 metres long which floods the lower floor of the pavilion: the WetLab. As you flow with the water down to the WetLab you enter an underwater world. Water drips from the walls and flows over the floor; as the wave fills the WetLab you experience the tidal movements of the sea. You are pushed back by the rising water level and have to wait for low tide before you can cross over to the other side. In the middle of the floor the water is drawn away. The changing colours of the dimmed lights reflect on the wet surfaces of the floor, walls and ceiling, creating an immersive underwater experience.

In this wet atmosphere the glowing Hydra is like giant seaweed. Sound travels through the Hydra, which is constantly changing colour. The sound is like a foreign language: you can follow the verbal flow but it remains incomprehensible. The Hydra is a continuous object: its multiple lines travel through the entire pavilion following the visitor; sometimes as

construction, sometimes as interface but always transmitting information by ways of light and sound. Within the Hydra there are multi-coloured fibre-optic cables and, every 2 metres, an active speaker system. All fibres and speakers are controlled by a central computer and react to visitors, changing weather conditions or pre-programmed algorithms.

Real worlds

After climbing out of the WetLab you approach a panoramic view of the surrounding landscape. At first, only a strip of sky is seen outside, then the horizon of the flat, Dutch delta landscape. Finally, you look down on and hover over the Oosterschelde sea. The panoramic window is the only place inside the pavilion which offers a view of the surroundings. The view is controlled by the airbag: an inflatable object that fits exactly in the opening of the window. When inflated it fills the entire space, closing the view. The closing and opening of the airbag is also controlled by the central computer – part of the overall programme of the pavilion.

Virtual water

After surveying the landscape you turn and walk on to the wave-floor and into the Sensorium. The wave-floor is the gigantic torsion-volume that divides the entire building body into two parts: the WetLab and the Sensorium.

In the Sensorium you are surrounded by all kinds of virtual representations of water. The five curved lines that stretch from one pole to the other correspond with the outer lines of the building body. Multi-coloured fibre-optic cable in these lines illuminate the Sensorium from behind the polycarbonate skin.

In both poles there is a set of red lights that is controlled by an interface in the Hydra. Pressing the interface causes the poles to be activated – to glow in bright red colours. The colour and dimming of the fibres is controlled by a series of sensorial parameters. The colour sequence is generated from bitmaps of all kinds of weather types taken from the Internet. The dimming of the fibres is controlled by the biorhythm of the building, which changes according to an algorithm that

has the weather conditions and water level outside of the building as its input.

In addition to the colour-scape there is a sound-scape in the Sensorium. Behind the polycarbonate skin there is an array of speakers which makes it possible for the sound to move dynamically through the space of the Sensorium.

The same interface that controls the lights in the polar regions allows the sound to be influenced. Sound samples can be added to the sound-scape by pressing the interface or pushing the sound towards a certain region in the Sensorium.

Virtual worlds
On both the surface of the wave-floor and the polycarbonate skin of the Sensorium can be seen see immersive projections of a series of virtual worlds. These all depict different perceptions of water or fluidity.

They are generated by two SGI o2 computers and their input comes from an interface that is integrated in the Hydra. With six high-resolution data projectors the worlds are projected on to the surface of the Sensorium. The six worlds are as follows: 1. *Ice* – the navigator moves through slowly pulsating ice masses; 2. *H_2O* – swarms of H_2O molecules flow through space. The navigator can travel with the swarm and try to catch a molecule; 3. *Life* – multiple intelligent creatures float in virtual space. The navigator attracts some of them while others are very shy; 4. *Blob* – a fluid mass is constantly deforming while the navigator floats around or through it; 5. *Flow* – the navigator is captured in a flow; 6. *Morph* – the navigator floats between two morphing sky-scapes. Due to the extreme wide-angle view the clouds rush by.

With these virtual worlds the building is extended into virtual space. The physical space continues seamless in virtual space. The navigator determines its own path and by doing so contributes to the sound- and colour-scape of the Sensorium.

The making: parametric design
To construct a design like the Salt Water Pavilion we had to develop a method that would maintain both absolute control and absolute flexibility during the construction period. We developed the concept of parametric design. Every inch of the building is different because of its fluid geometry. With this particular design method we describe the fluidly varying lines of the building volume in terms of parameters.

To stay in control both economically and aesthetically, we constructed a three-dimensional database that was linked to the three-dimensional model. From this database was generated the data for every specific participant in the building process. The builder received only a few principal details together with various tables concerning the parametric values. This data was used sometimes directly as input for CNC machines and at other times used on the building site.

Parametric design enabled us to stay in control of the building concept that we developed for the Salt Water Pavilion. Instead of fixing the building in two-dimensional drawings it was able to remain liquid within its three-dimensional database.

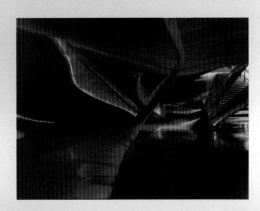

Knox Architects, Salt Water Pavilion, interior views

*Exterior views showing position related
to Salt Water Pavilion*

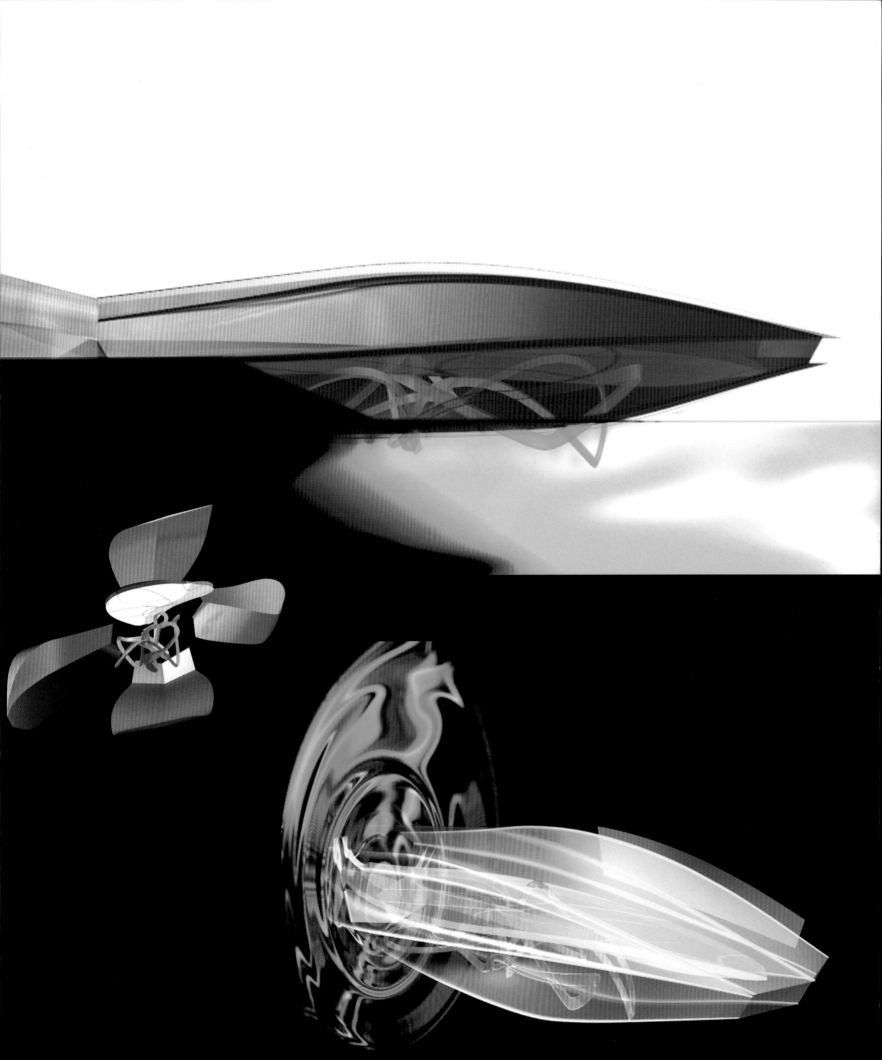

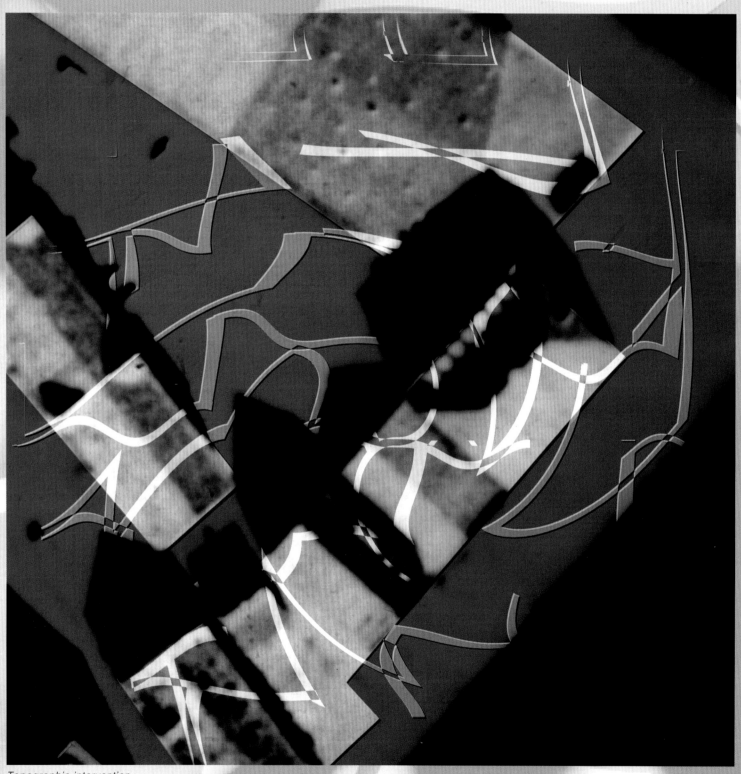

Topographic intervention

STUDIO ASYMPTOTE

ARCHITEXTURING COPENHAGEN
Hani Rashid and Lise Anne Couture

Texture mapping is a process available to us today with the aid of computer imaging. The texture map (which is essentially the incorporation of an image, text or pattern overlaid or superimposed on to or within any other computer-generated surface, construct or image) reveals an array of potential readings or misreadings. This is by no means entirely different to the traditions of collage, or in the case of film, that of montage. It is however significant in its distinction from these other mechanisms, in so far as it integrates by means of dispersion and difference as opposed to the collagist's methodology of combination by similitude and the erasure of the seam.

A texture-mapped surface or entity is essentially one made up of simultaneously distinct yet morphologically integrated components and reveals, as a result of its own processes, an immanence of structure and possibility.

Procedures
– Subject the city plan of Copenhagen to an external and impartial device, thereby isolating various unexpected sites for possible intervention. Each of these 'overlooked' territories contains latent architecture and programmes that may be brought to the fore by means of a series of chance texture-mapping operations.
– Texture maps are formulated according to certain 'field operations' retrieved from the combination of maze and labyrinth mathematical strategies. Each resultant construct is then integrated within the aerial photographs (surveillances) of the various sites determined by the overlay of the UTM grid.
– These combined images reveal potential strategies for architectural interventions within the residual territories made apparent through aerial surveillance.
– Programmes are integrated through another set of chance operations, this time retrieved from a tourist source, assuming that tourists will always locate the overlooked sites although they may not necessarily acknowledge their presence. These sites, therefore, contain an immanent architecture that through a slight adjustment of one's comprehension might be transformed into actual sites of spectacle and revelatory sites of appreciation (ie tourist attractions).

Perspective

FROM ABOVE: Dummy caption, dummy

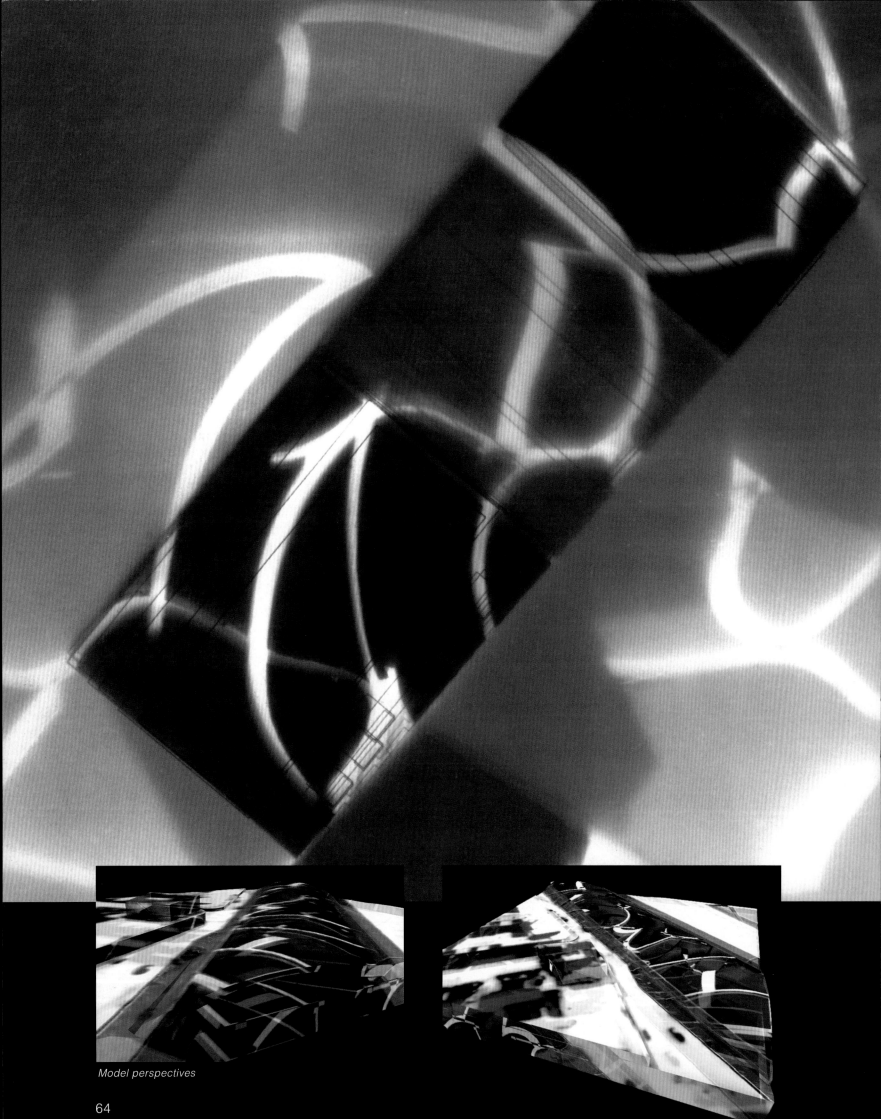

Model perspectives

64

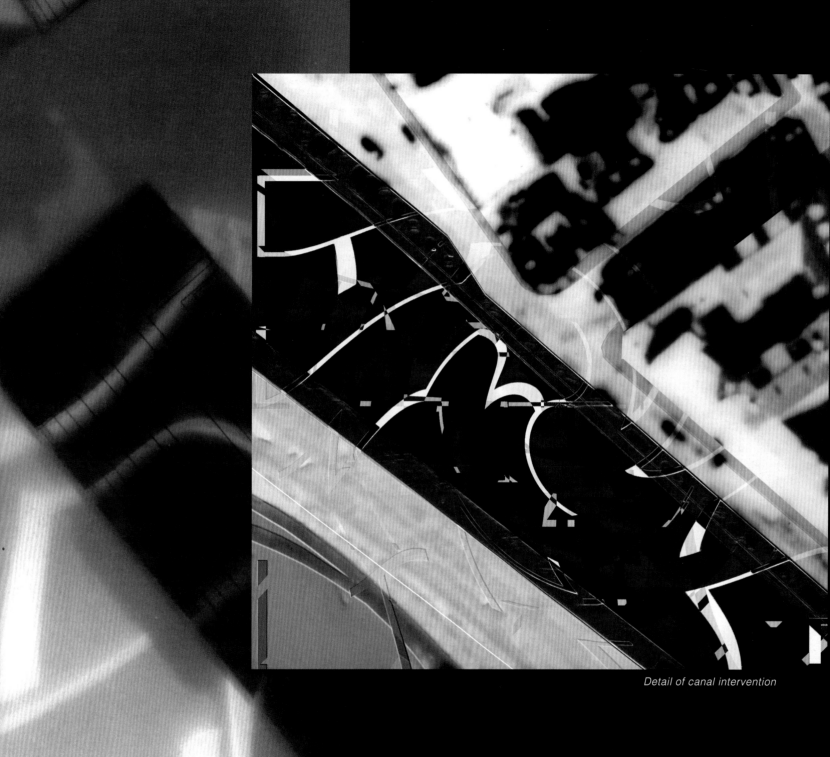

Detail of canal intervention

BERNARD CACHE/OBJECTILE
TOPOLOGICAL ARCHITECTURE AND THE AMBIGUOUS SIGN

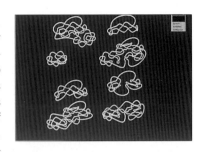

The work of Objectile (Bernard Cache, Patrick Beaucé, and Taoufik Hammoudi) utilises design strategies situated within contemporary modes of production as a means to effect critical practices. Cache's development of the implicit relevance that materiality and fabrication have for architecture is significant, derived from the thought of Gilles Deleuze: particularly with respect to topology, the fold and planes of immanence. In *The Fold*, Deleuze refers specifically to Bernard Cache, a theorist in his own right; the closest evidence perhaps of Deleuze's proximity to architecture.[1]

Cache's theories are a rigorous source of what may be called the 'topologising' of architecture: a trajectory that is disseminating within the architectural field, not only as a result of the increasing presence of computer technology but due to the increasing complexity of contemporary life. It is ironic, yet interesting, that Cache's applications and implementations put the issue of authorship in architecture at risk.

Drawing upon a variety of scales and design problems, Cache's theories have reworked the classical tenets of architecture, stemming from Vitruvian theory with its basis in Platonic form. Translating Deleuze's rereading of Leibniz and the Baroque, Cache reworks the fundamental geometry of architecture: substituting the square, circle and triangle, with the frame, vector and inflection, which have tremendous import through their generative dynamics, in contradistinction to the combinatory logic of Platonic forms.

Cache's fundamental argument that all form consists of either convex or concave curvature, stems from his analysis of inflection – what Leibniz calls an 'ambiguous sign'. For Cache, an inflection has the characteristics of a geometric undecidable, which works outwardly from its centre. This is defined as an 'intrinsic singularity'.[2] The inflection works in a generative way, disseminating a geologic of openness and responsiveness to the potentials of an encounter.

Cache translates the fundamental dynamics of curvature, situated between the earth and the sky, describing topological relationships between geography and architecture, inside and landscape: filtered through a complex double frame. This is reflected most clearly in his furniture designs which are predominately of wood, exploiting the inherent contours of the material. Much of the work of Bernard Cache and

Objectile is achieved through computer milling. Computer programming is just one of the many sites of inquiry of this philosopher, mathematician and businessman, whose theories are also insinuated in information technology. Cache has evaluated three computer-modelling paradigms that effect the discipline of architecture; one of which, he insists, architects have not, as yet, considered. While well-known to architectural practice, the dominant softwares are specifically avoided for being too inflexible.

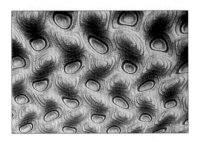

At the other end of the spectrum is the higher-end, animation software. Although this is easily capable of creating fluid forms based upon animation and radical deformation, it is not geared towards full-scale fabrication. Instead, Cache chooses to rework software which is more familiar to industrial designers, who create precise components for mass production. It is the 'exact-modelling' software environment, Cache argues, that has the greatest potential for architectural variegation. This represents an interesting alternative to much of the content in this volume on hypersurface theory, whereby radical image-forms generated by high-end computers translate algorithmic data into complex configurations, exemplified by the work of Marcos Novak.

The overall objective of hypersurface theory is to allow for Other forces – cultural forces or subtle, sub-dominant forces – to influence, determine and destabilise the pure authority of the author/architect. The exact modelling of Cache's work is an interesting foray into an already dominant mode of production (manufacturing industries), where the generation of materialised form is determined by profit motivated, consumer-driven corporations. The mainstream corporation is what Cache, in his most Marxist moment, seeks to displace. Therefore Cache's work is, indeed, a strategy that calls into question the dominant powers, but by working within these powers seeks to challenge them, as close to the heart of the tradition as is possible (hence his close reading of Vitruvius).[3] This raises the issue of how other practices interpret the complexities of the contemporary world and how one may work within that complexity to further its chaosmotic potential.[4]

The ability of Cache's middle-range, modified software to produce the necessary tolerance for industrial design production is significant: taking

FROM ABOVE: Algorithmic knots; artificial landscape; non-standard bistro table

what used to be the parameters of the Industrial Revolution and mass production and reworking the systemic to accommodate infinite variation. This procedure has the potential to reconfigure a determinant that has a considerable impact on our built environment. Even though this places Cache's modus operandi on a middle scale, in terms of architecture (furniture, body, ornament and so forth), it is here that he establishes an important connection between Deleuze and Guattari's theories of indeterminacy and the very forces of capitalism; and here that he locates a critical schema within an inhabitable plane of immanence.

Cache is intent upon forging a direct connection between the multiplicity of consumer desire and the dominant modes of production that drive capitalism. He wants the mode of production to be placed in the hands of the consumer, a tactic that presents a significant challenge to the corporations of sameness that shape cultural identity. His interest here is in liberating the consumer from the repressive forces of consumer culture, seeking instead to celebrate alterability that can become an inherent feature within aggregate production.

Cache wishes to maximise the flexibility and variability available within the mode of production; an ability that goes much further than mere self-determination. If infinite variegation is a fact of production, then identity as such is rendered in a far more complex way, leading us back to Cache's theories of Subjectiles and Objectiles. The scope of these theories is extensive, offering a substantial contribution to a theory of hypersurfaces.[5] His most recent project for a Textile Museum is outlined as follows.

Notes

1 Gilles Deleuze, *The Fold: Leibniz and the Baroque*, Tom Conley (trans), University of Minnesota Press (Minneapolis), 1993, p14.

2 Bernard Cache, *Earth Moves: The Furnishing of Territories* Michael Speaks (ed), Anne Boyman (trans), The MIT Press (Cambridge, Mass), 1995, p34.

3 Bernard Cache presented a lecture at Columbia University during the Fall of 1997, where he unfolded a specific attachment to and interrogation of Vitruvian theory. A transcript of that lecture is to appear in the forthcoming, *Columbia Documents of Architecture and Theory*, vol 7.

4 Félix Guattari, *Chaosmosis: An Ethico-Aesthetic Paradigm*, Paul Bains and Julian Pefanis (trans), The University of Indiana Press (Bloomington), 1995.

5 Ibid, p92; in particular, his discussion of half-object, half-subject.

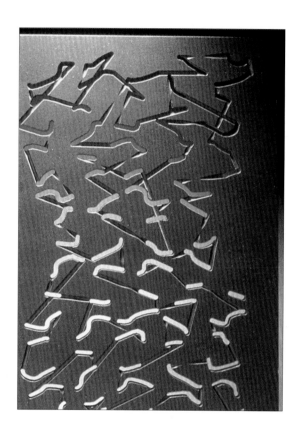

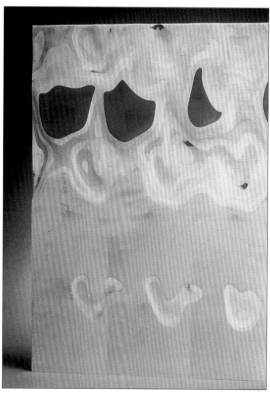

FROM ABOVE: Acoustic wood panel; decorative wood panel

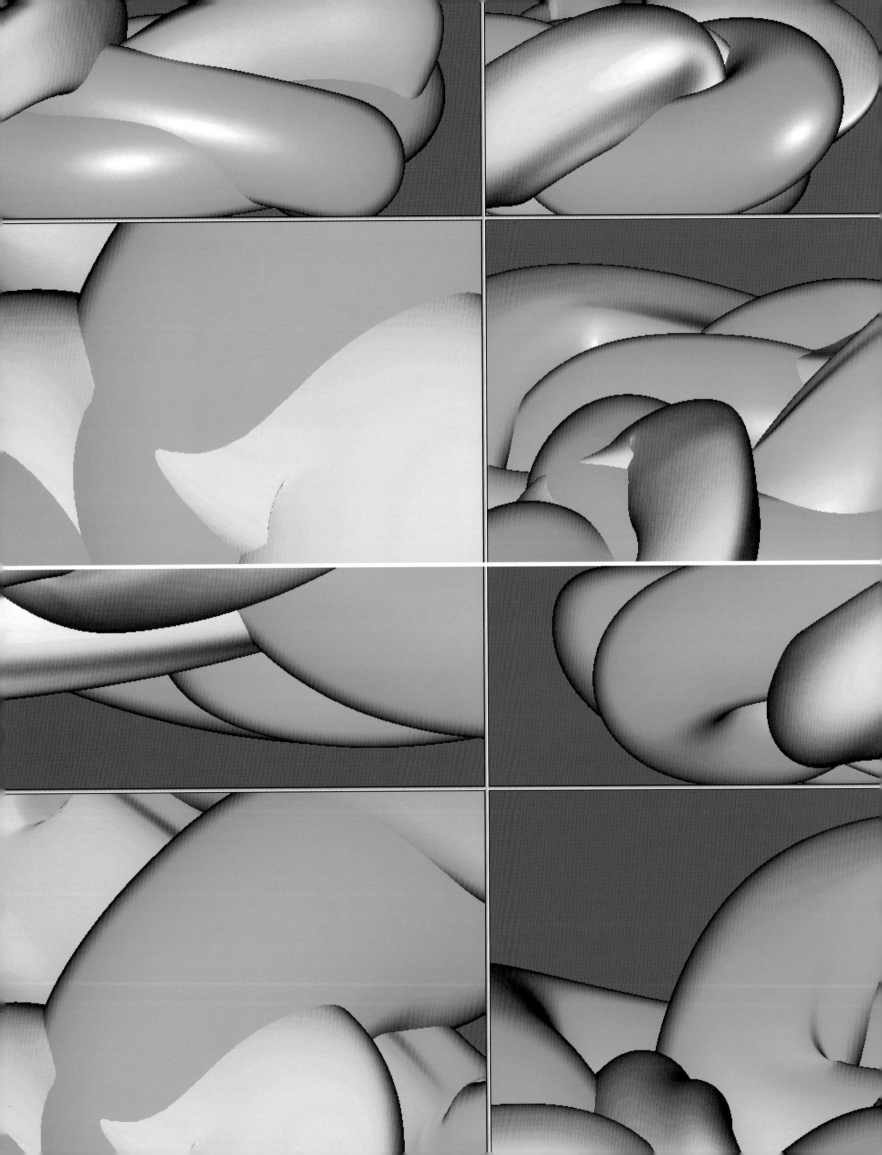

Textile Museum

This project investigates knot and string theory, questioning how a knot can be obtained when the inflexion loops onto itself, or how to escape from organicism when the open surface closes itself to form a solid. The question arises from the structure of the mathematical functions we use when we design 'objectiles' as opposed to 'subjectiles'.

In a Semperian mode, structure is subordinated to cladding. Thus textile technology comes prior to tectonics, ceramics and stereotomy.
The key element of textile is the knot. Our software development of knot generation provides very different results starting with traditional patterns, ie Arabic, Celtic, and so forth, and then developing them further with Penrose spatial structures, and then finally becoming the building itself.

Knot models are being used in various human sciences. For Gottfried Semper the knot was much more than just a technical element: it deals with a basic sense of corporeity, hence our detailed images. However, these images also allow us to study architectural detailing, like the lines of intersection between the several interlacing elements. The knot also works on the architectural pattern of the patio, which until now we considered as a horizontal torus. With the use of an interlace the different patios are perceived as overlapping one another.

Such architecture can only be built with the support of good non-standard technologies. The interesting problem of establishing a horizontal floor within this building may be considered.

Finally, this knot architecture plan seems particularly well suited to a museum with different sections. These can become circuits which are bifurcated at the crossings.

Stephen Perrella

*OPPOSITE: Details of intersections;
RIGHT, FROM ABOVE: Front elevation;
side elevation; plan*

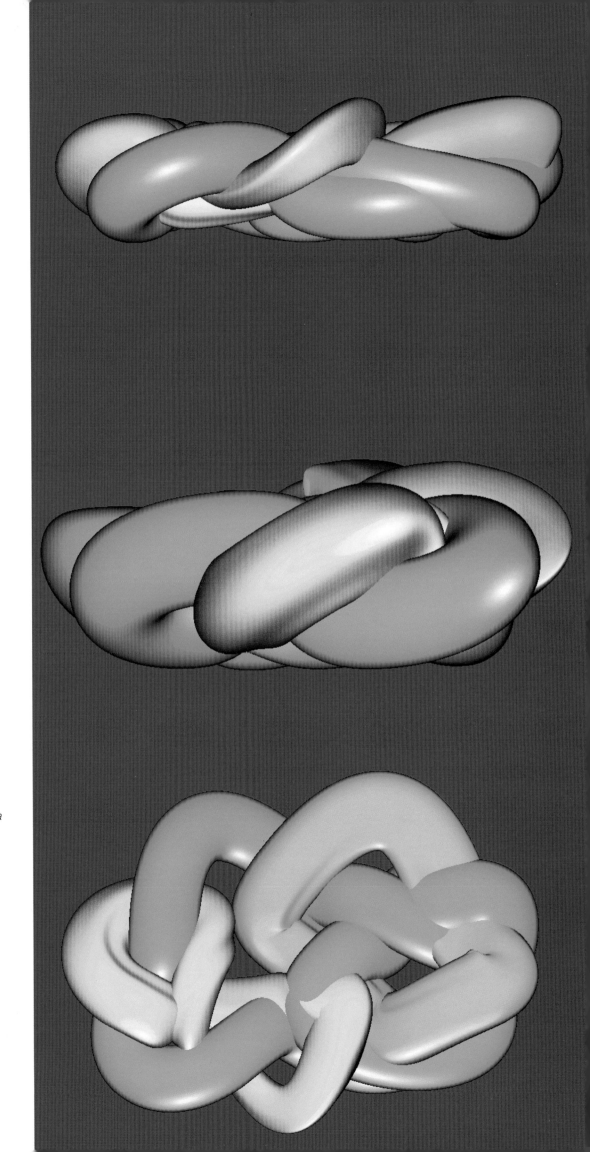

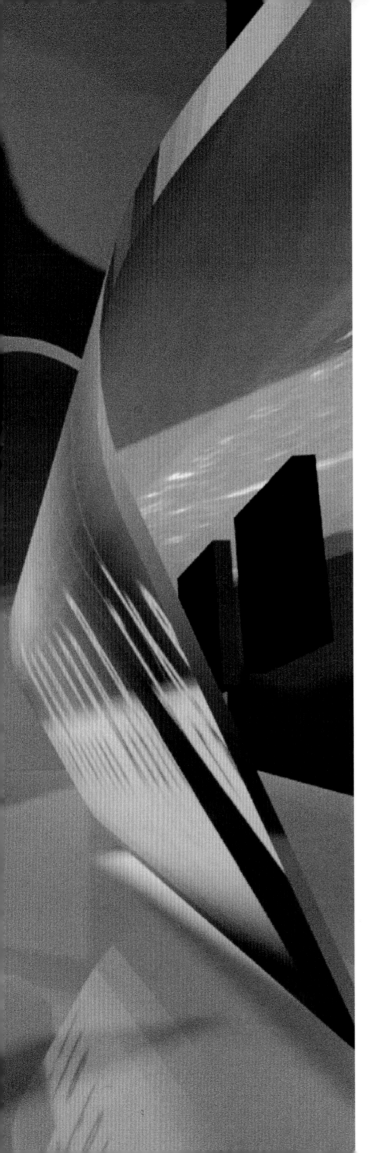

VAN BERKEL & BOS
REAL SPACE IN QUICK TIMES PAVILION
Milan Triennale

The computer is a way of radically breaking with traditional design processes. The mediation techniques enabled by the computer signify a complete overthrow of many architectural assumptions, from the typology of organisational structures, to the hierarchical order of planning a structure, ending with the details. The computer entails a radical rethinking of the valuations implicit in architectural design. In this sense, computational techniques could represent the first important development in architecture since modernism.

The architecture of this pavilion, exhibited in 1996, evolves from a series of projects developed by Van Berkel & Bos which reflect the increasing importance of computer techniques in the design process. The computer entails a new approach to architecture as it negates the prioritisation of the object; aspects of the tactile programme and of the surroundings are thrown in unequivocally. In this sense, the computer is indifferent to what it is fed; all information is equal. As a result, internal influences and external forces become the unprejudiced instruments towards the materialisation of the project.

One of the notable features of a design process steered by CAD is that information changes the output, which changes the

OPPOSITE AND OVERLEAF: Computer images

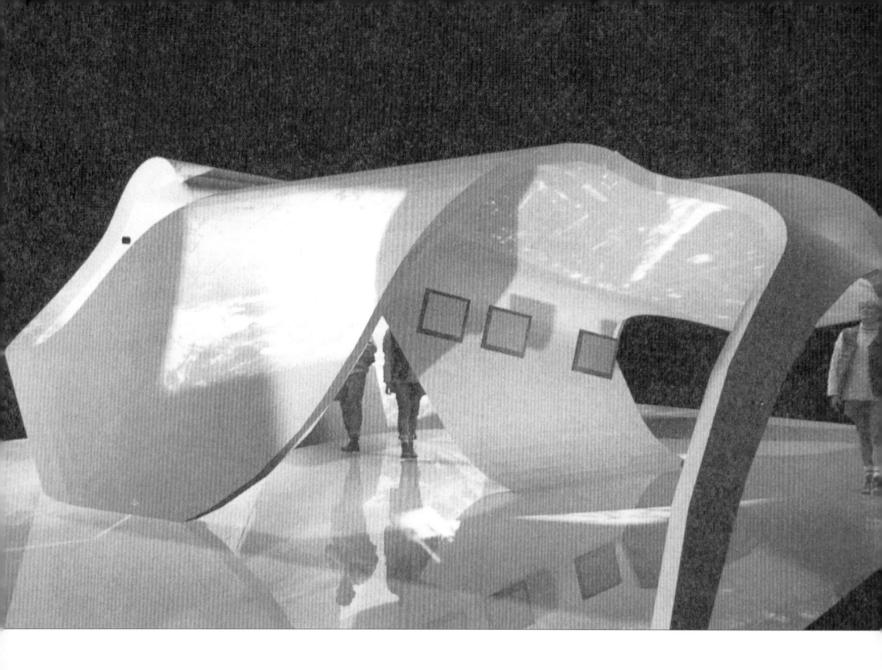

input, and so on; the crux of this type of transvaluation is that everything becomes unfixed, floating or liquid. This 'wave-like' process contains the real interest of computational techniques, as exemplified in the pavilion.

Structuring with the computer sheds new light on the identity of structure itself. Recently, a fresh view has emerged of structures as process fields of materialisations, based on spatial shifting devices, rather than representing any homogeneous, linear system. Structures are losing their specific, separate properties and are defined more by how they relate to the organisation of the whole and how you relate to them: you zoom in to solids, you fluctuate along evanescent distances, space opens up around you; any variety of mutations is possible, all unquantifiable, orderless, dimensionless, happening as in a fluidum.

This is the type of structure that shapes the pavilion. The confined room of the exhibition space, measuring 9 x 9 metres, is expanded with the aid of the amorphous, shell-like structure which represents many different qualities. The structure is the carrier of the exhibition, incorporating a digital and a virtual space; it reflects projections and organises the space.

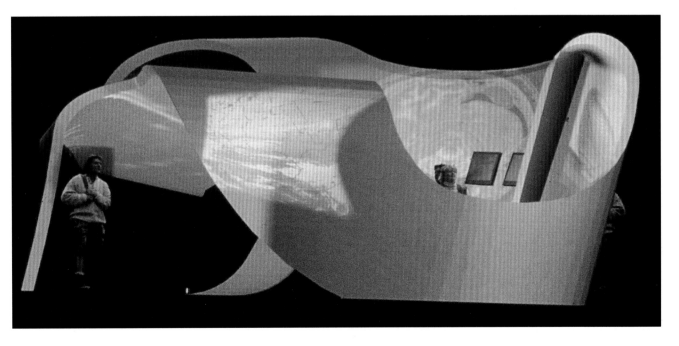

FROM ABOVE: Théâtre Oblique
dans une structure, *1972;* Surface
en X, *1966*

CLAUDE PARENT

THE OBLIQUE FUNCTION MEETS ELECTRONIC MEDIA

My approach as an architect was characterised, as early as 1950, by the professional interest I had in the media at the time (in particular with the collaboration of Ionel Schein). This approach towards the press and cinema, and later towards television, was so unusual that it has been criticised by my peers. One should not forget that in France, in the 1950s, it was forbidden by the Architects' Chapter to sign a building or to publicise one's work in a way that would give its presentation a commercial quality.

Therefore, right from the beginning, I was not well accepted by my professional colleagues as an architect who publicised his work and his ideas with the support of the press; quite laughable, I suppose, to the eyes of the Anglo-Saxons. Magazines like *Elle*; *Paris Match*; François Lazaroff's group *France Soir*; *Jardin des modes*; *Science et vie*; *Realités*; *Plaisirs de France*; *Femina*, and of course *Architecture d'Aujourd'hui* – in addition to the art press – became champions of my work, and moreover, keys to opening my mind to architecture and projecting my ideas towards the future.

My research was influenced very early on by its relationship to the world of news through the popular press and by a fusion with the artistic world via André Bloc.

The study of the 'Spaciodynamic City' with sculptor Nicolas Schöffer in 1954 is an idiosyncratic example of this mind-set. 'Utopian City' (1954) was certainly related to the 1917 Russian Constructivists' essays/experiments but it already linked up with all kinds of communication systems expressed by architecture up to its theoretical limits.

A 1955 project consisted of the realisation of a full-sized model at the 'Construction Show'. This depicted the way in which the facades of buildings, instead of being simple enclosures, would interact like real urban transmitters, allowing for exchanges, as permanent sources of information creating animation in the city.

Nicolas Schöffer and myself had already realised image screens projected on to mobile sculptures on commercial billboards, and through this 'light dynamism' we were to create alive and expressive facades of the spacio-dynamic city which would become 'cybernetic'.

Finally, however, the press group originally interested in this urban setting of information withdrew because of all the technical problems. In fact, our demands were too advanced for the ambitions and state of the media at that time.

The power and the wealth of the written press prevented them from anticipating the transformation that we were witnessing. A transformation as rapid as it was unavoidable. The important fact to remember was that in 1955 an architect and a sculptor had tried to create an architecture in close relation to the development of the media.

At the same time, Nicolas Schöffer designed the 'Key Hole' House which subjected visitors to a 'cold' space and a 'hot' space communicated through pictorial and dynamic means which did not need to be interpreted intellectually by visitors. The information was sufficient to enable understanding by all visitors, whether educated or uneducated.

Ten years later with Paul Virilio, we dealt with this problem in a different way through our proposal of 'inclined planes' or the oblique. The foundation of life was not neutral any longer but active, and the disruption caused by the inclined plane could not be misunderstood since it was addressed to obvious human attitudes like balance and imbalance (stability, instability, shift of references). It used indisputable means of direct information such as tactility. The non-coded 'foot' and the non-coded 'hand' also became foremost and unquestionable information sources and superseded the eye and the logical intelligence, which are considered usual filters of the understanding of space.

In order to explain the introduction of 'topology' into the discourse on space (to the detriment of form which at this point in time was predominant), I took a simple and ordinary tactile image which has never been appreciated by architects. I said that architecture was like knitwear, that one would start the sweater at one end and would finish it at the other extremity without defining its limits.

This prosaic way to consider space in its continuity and in its deformation was too natural to be convincing, although it was extremely genuine as well as popular. I continually reasserted that the oblique was not an architecture proposing a new language, but rather a tool. This approach always prompts fresh is-

FROM ABOVE: La Carapace – surface en X, *1966;* Sur-face/Sous-face, *1972;* Théâtre Oblique, *1972*

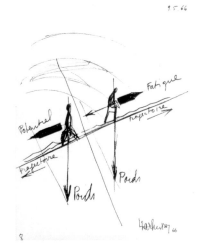

sues to be raised, leading to the discovery of new solutions and relations to the space, and finally the creation of new spaces which would have been unimaginable through traditional methods of creation.

This part of the research has been denied by French architects, and this is where the sadness lies in not having been understood. However, I am convinced that as a result of the dazzling development of contemporary electronic media that we have witnessed, and the newness and power of means that researchers benefit from today, the oblique is gaining the place it originally deserved.

It is linked naturally to the research that Stephen Perrella calls Hypersurface. One of the paths that the oblique had hoped to explore was the notion of limit, a notion which now becomes important when exploring topology. The oblique had explored the absolute necessity of a threshold of restoration when one wants to pass from, or more exactly jumps from, one continuity to another. In mathematics there is the notion of solution of continuity which allows, while breaking up mathematical space, for the passage of one element to another within the continuity of a topological space and thus, despite the excessive deformations of space.

Let us not forget that architecture lives only in the revelation of the limits it conceives. In the past, the wall was its recurrent image. The

adventurer was the one who pushed away limits of knowledge; who moved away the wall.

As a result of electronic media, the architect experiences spaces which were never conceived before. He discovers them and at the same time pushes away the limits of form. The 'media' wall still remains to be invented as a modern notion of 'enclosure' which undoubtedly will include the intervention of time.

Meanwhile, let us hope that Hypersurface architects opt for good choices within the infinity of possibilities that the new technology of the machine can offer them. In any case, whatever the resulting quality, it should be acknowledged that electronic media enabled new methodologies to be invented, and that it is only through such imaginative approaches that one will be able to improve architecture. Without a fresh approach, it is not possible for creation to be improved.

The relevance of the computer tool we use, thanks to the strength of today's new technologies, directly stimulates our 'imagination' – to a point that it could help solve a fundamental question which seemed insoluble: how one can keep the modern quality of continuity ('vanishing spaces') and preserve the ancestral notion of enclosure ('limit'). How shall one make these two architectural poles reconcilable?

Translated by Laetitia Wolff

Important note

Important in our understanding of the 'oblique function' is that for the first time it has substituted the notion of surface for one of volume in the definition of space.

Thus, in relation to the 'oblique function' one cannot speak about interior and exterior, or of enclosure-envelope realising the distinction, one could say the discrimination, between internal space and external space. This distinction describes architecture through the limits between the two, and thus whatever ingenuity an architect needs to make it as non-existent as possible (Richard Neutra for instance), even virtual (actuality).

In the oblique function, this research around the notion of enclosure which had agitated the architectural milieu does not need to be, because it does not exist. Indeed, the enclosure is linked to the notion of volume (distinction container-content) whereas the oblique function materialises the structure of space, by the surface under and over, both creating more or less parallel layers, whose meeting and interpenetration creates limits allowing for the inhabitability and the use of these surfaces.

Everything resides in this major principle of the oblique function. There is no such thing as interior (circulation) and exterior (shelter) but an ensemble of surfaces developed and associated so that, while creating a coverable totality, they determine endless protected surfaces or open-air surfaces ('inhabitable circulation').

The word limit is therefore wrong because it is unadapted. One has to invent a new word, a novel expression to define the progressive penetration towards protection, the fact that enclosure is not formulated architecturally by a specific element but becomes virtual, imprecise, indecisive, maybe even a tangibly and not illusory virtual through the transparency of glass: an illusion.

Historical note

From the 1920s throughout the 1930s, there was an attempt to destroy volume via the decomposition and *mise en scène* of plans (Rietveld). However, imprisoned in the orthogonal (and in its constraining system), the attempt was limited to an aesthetic change and never reached further than a fashion, whereas in fact it dealt with a very innovative doctrinal point. What a pity!

FROM ABOVE: Les Grandes Oreilles, *1966;* Premier croquis sur le Potentialisme, *1966;* Untitled, *1970; OPPOSITE:* Intérieur, *1973;* Espace de Rencontre, *1973*

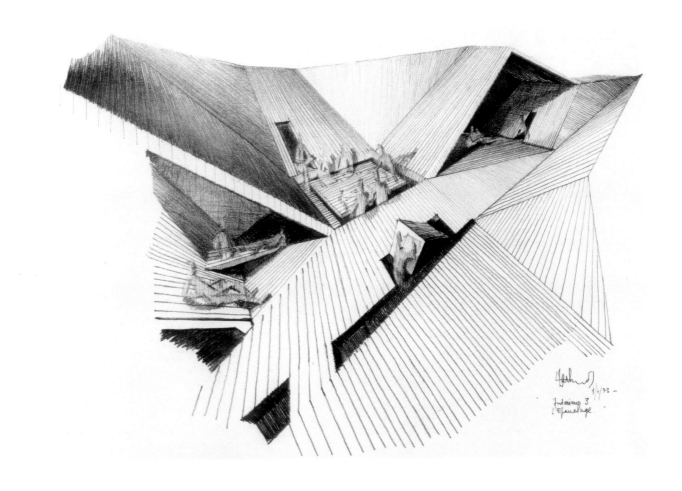

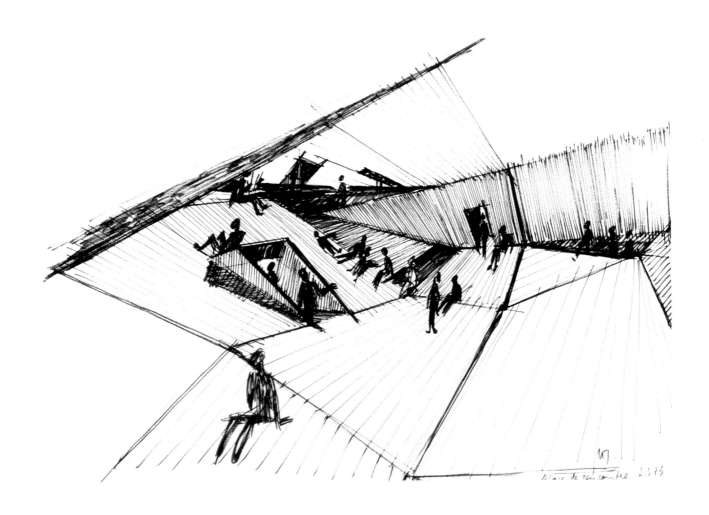

STEPHEN PERRELLA WITH DENNIS PANG
THE HAPTIC HORIZON

This diagram shows how a new mixture of electronic horizons configures an 'infrastructure'; not a literal infrastructure, in the sense of transportation routes and backbones for distribution, but a diagram for new modalities of human agency, one that supersedes a now outmoded Cartesian paradigm. This is constituted of seams and interstitial folds resulting in fluxing lines of demarcation, converting separate realms into grafted ones. Once a virtual dimension appears, the provisional layers of existing fabric implode, engendering fluid inter-permutations. Our cultural 'ground' becomes a continuous zone of inflections whereby the 'real' is subject to fluxation and interfoldings into a systemic of dynamic interrelations; a systemic of transversality. The effects of this condition erupt from very specific machinations within praxis, not outside it. There is no outside or inside.

In our existing context there are horizons through which our lives are drawn. The emergence of a virtual dimension attenuates a further layer beyond two current electronic strata. Respectively they are the: 'Free Space Horizon', the 'Signification-Infrastructure Horizon' and most recently, the 'Internetted Horizon'. Combined, these three horizons organise layers of activity or inhabitation but should not be considered mutually exclusive.

Increasingly, capitalism drives a world culture of consumption forcing these layers to become more dense and interwoven. The process and logic of pervasion stemming from teletechnology intermixes television within the Internet, the Internet impacts upon built infrastructure, and so forth, creating a convergent, infolded, organisation. From this condensed condition arise new and emergent phenomena. The action of this schema seems to occur from the middle out. For instance, it was originally thought that the electronic revolution would replace print media. But instead what has actually happened is that the virtual dimension has increased and saturated the media even further. From this construct, specific relationships may be understood as hypersurfaces, a term that attempts to characterise the complex way new interfaces will occur and reconfigure us.

Within this three-tiered interpretation of technologised culture, what critical dynamic brings about the virtual dimension? It seems historically that the middle layer, the electronic infrastructure, packed with programs of communications, adverts, print media, telephonic discourse, transportation, commerce and all of the other trappings of an industrialised and post-industrialised infrastructure, is an urban society that operates as a plane of immanence.

With the advent of television in the early 1950s, another layer is generated out from the 'middle', seeming to be above the metropolis, extending beyond and creating a vast sub-urban terrain, where the logic of broadcast media effects a generalised narratological simultaneity controlled by the military industrial complex. Its effect on culture is closer to social engineering, as the spread of advertisement and entertainment stand in place of meaningful social discourse. With the advent of free-space there is no possibility for a non-mediated dialogue.

These interpenetrating layers, fuelled by consumer capitalism will reconfigure the topology of human agency. Emergent forms of representation will unfold due to the radical interweavings, creating both commensurate and incommensurate juxtapositions of varying fields. This condition may perhaps be best understood as a surrealism imbedded within the everyday. The way that it will effect the architecture/culture mix is being taken up under a thematic called Hypersurface, and may be what results from the exigencies of the virtual dimension.

The Haptic Horizon, 1995, was a speculative project exploring emergent superpositions (seams) between background surfaces imbricated with animated texture maps containing sequences from popular culture cinema. Using these sequences within an architectural project, its context and the 'world' containing these entities, connected each – form, context and supercontext – into an interwoven informational continuity – a haptic horizon

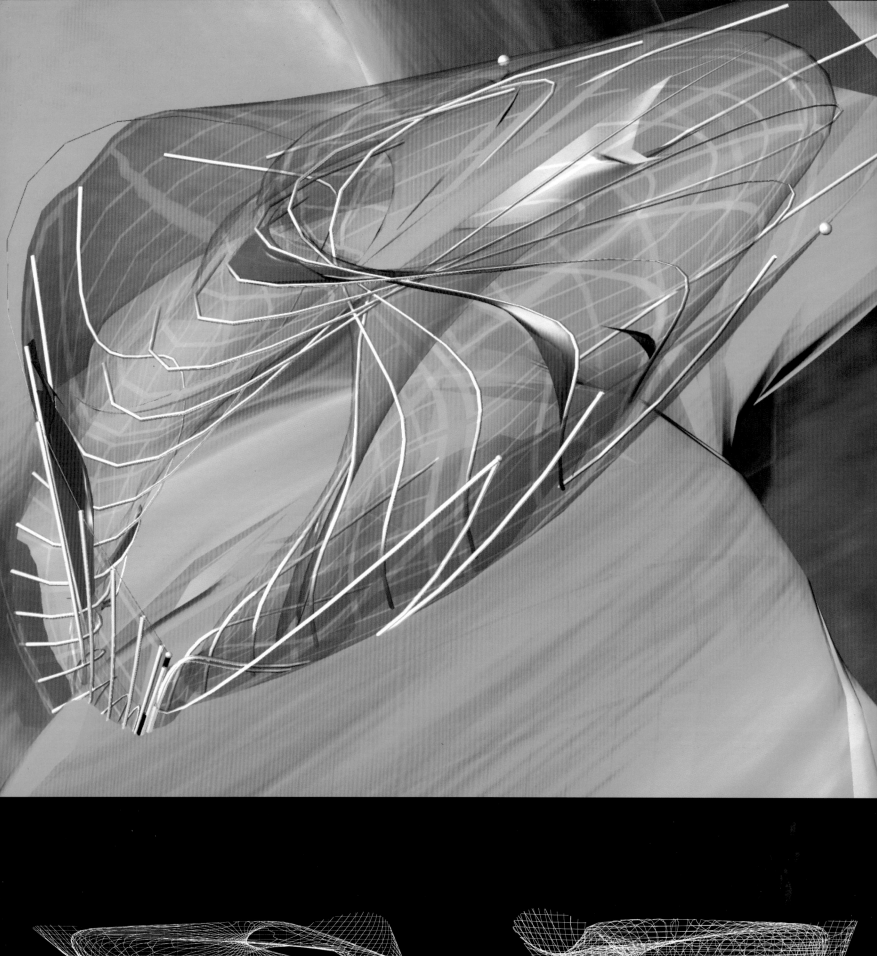
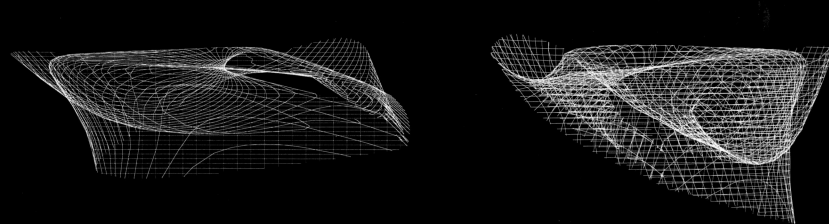

STEPHEN PERRELLA WITH REBECCA CARPENTER
THE MÖBIUS HOUSE STUDY

This study (1997-98) is an investigation into contemporary domesticity to reconsider dwelling for the new millennium. A preliminary analysis revealed that the pervasive use of technology in the home presents an ontological dilemma. Current house formats are no longer tenable because space and time are reconfigured by a lived informational geometry. Dwelling has become problematic solely in terms of Euclidean space as a result of media infiltrations – a force that implodes distance and then perplicates subjectivity as it enfolds viewer perception into an endless barrage of electronic images. This occurs in combination with, and yet is dissimilar to, the dynamics of teletechnology and computer-to-Internet connectivity. As home-viewing narrows onto the TV surface, it fuses with an image-blitz into a perpetual present.[1] Teletechnology contributes to a burrowing effect, altering the home as an exclusively interior condition. This battlefield of intersubjectivity problematises the dweller-consumer as an ego-construct-identity, traditionally based upon an interiority divided from an exteriority and governed by an ideality.

The Möbius House study diagram for post-Cartesian dwelling is thus neither an interior space nor an exterior form. It is a transversal membrane that reconfigures binary notions of interior/exterior into a continuous, interwrapping median – it is a hypersurface. The current phase of the study presents a fluxing diagram-membrane generated by an animated inflection. It is a hypersurface generated by first deconstructing the supporting geometry of a NURB (non-uniform rational B-spline) curve in the animation software by Microsoft/Softimage. Each singular control point that governs a five-point NURB was animated along the path of a Möbius surface, generating a topology that cannot be understood by either Euclidean or Cartesian geometry. Within the animation sequences, temporal delays are programmed to avoid determinate, linear form: what is otherwise known as 'the stopping problem'.[2] The Möbius House study is thus irreducible, rendering it open to complex, temporal experience: it is architecture that is not based upon fundamental form or space and therefore, in part, constitutive of experience; not an attempt to contain or act as a plane of reference. It is a transversal construct.[3] A domestic hypersurface program thus emerges immanently from the diagram-substrate, facilitating proprioceptive experience, a radical empiricism more commensurate with the complexities of new-millennial modes of inhabitation.[4]

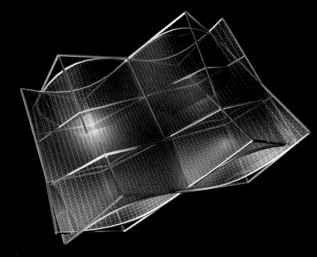

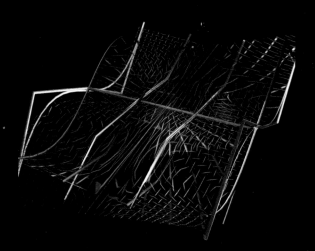

Notes
1 In *Blue Sky* (Verso, 1997) Paul Virilio discusses the notion of pyknoleptic from pyknolepsy, a medical term denoting childhood avsence epilepsy.
2 In the 'Emerging Complexities' Symposium at Columbia University GSAP, Spring 1997, theorist-economist Akira Asada raised the issue of whay he called the 'stopping problem' – a way of describing work that attempts to bring temporality into architectural form. He noted that at a certain phase of design development, the form must be frozen and then conceivably built as such. Hypersurface theory and the Möbius House study

argue that if the constituting or governing structures of form are considered separately from a lived program, then 'animate' form will exist only in the realm of materiality. What is most significant about the work of Deleuze and Guattari is that they ofer a means to evacuate such dualities.
3 See Gary Genosko's essay in this volume, pp32-37.
4 See Brian Massumi's essay in this volume, pp16-25. His thesis on proprioperception entails an enrichment of experience that embraces but reworks the impoverishing dynamics within the schizophrenia that stems from capitalism.

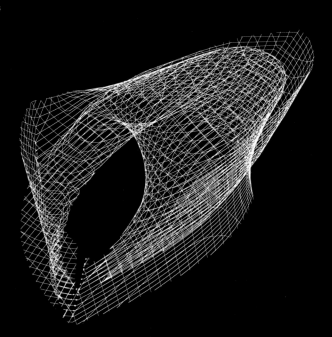

OPPOSITE: X, Y, Z sections; FROM ABOVE: Hypersurface panel studies 1 and 2; X, Y Z axonometric

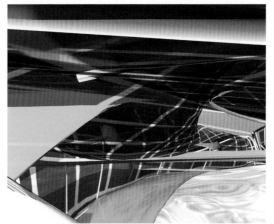

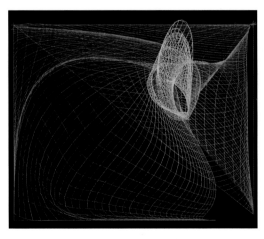 

MARCOS NOVAK

TRANSARCHITECTURES AND HYPERSURFACES
Operations of Transmodernity

Transmodernity: becoming alien

After modernity, virtuality: all that is solid melts into information. Between modernity and virtuality, transmodernity. As we all know, definitions, disciplines, institutions have all become unstable and inadequate, and everywhere there are re-evaluations of the structures by which we comprehend the world. These changes are not formless. They are characterised by the aspects of metamorphic change clustered under the prefix 'trans': transformation, transmutation, transgression, etc. Everywhere present, this kind of change is most evident in the structures of our quest for knowledge.

Historically, guilds became epistemes, specialisations and disciplines only to reach an impasse of isolations. In stages, their boundaries softened, merged and collapsed. From separate disciplines (degree zero) we ventured to multidisciplinarity (degree one), interdisciplinarity (degree two) and finally transdisciplinarity (degree three), spawning new sciences rooted in, but utterly unlike, previous explorations. Like the situation that arises in the collision of black holes, the event horizons of separate views on the world touched, merged and became one, but not merely as a Hegelian synthesis of thesis and antithesis moving onto some next 'higher level', but as a metamorphosis into conditions that are unprecedented rungs on the ladder, taking us from a centuries-long outlook called modernity to another stage called virtuality. In-between modernity and virtuality spans the transversal link we are crossing: transmodernity.

Firstly, every path, bridge or ladder fulfils a role of passage, but simple linear movement is not yet full 'transport' in that it merely propels something along a single, unaltered and unchallenged line of development, providing incremental progress without qualitative change. Transmodernity is not about incremental progress but about transformative exponential change. Secondly, some transmissions occur not as simple linear sequences, but as operations of multi-threading: transversal weavings and warpings of initially disparate strands. It is the proliferation of these conditions of transversal weaving and warping which characterises transmodernity. Thirdly, these admixtures result in conditions that are not merely collages or juxtapositions, as would characterise modernity, nor morphings, blendings or folds, nor even formations of monstrosities that are still terrestrial, as would characterise recent postmodernity, but transmutations into unpredictable conceptual spaces, completely new states of being. This is, of course, very rhizomic and could be described in terms of lines of flight, de- and re-territorialisations, and the full conceptual mechanism of 'A Thousand Plateaus'.[1] This is no surprise: transmodernity is about becoming: becoming *alien*.

Conceivable/presentable

In his essay 'Answer to the Question: What is the Postmodern?' Jean-François Lyotard posits that both modernity and postmodernity are responses to the problem of 'the sublime relationship between the presentable and the conceivable'.[2] He mentions two responses, varying by where they place the accent of the failure to make the conceivable and the presentable coincide. On the one hand, 'the accent can fall on the inadequacy of the faculty of presentation'; on the other hand, 'the accent can fall on the power of the faculty to conceive, on what one might call its 'inhumanity'. Modernity, he claims, is a nostalgic invocation of the Kantian sublime as absent content, while postmodernity is a concession to the pain and pleasure of inexpressibility but a refusal of the nostalgia of correct form.

The transmodern stance I am articulating takes a different position. Whereas Lyotard's positions both assume the 'human' as fixed, transmodernity accepts as given the technological augmentation of the human, either as the cyborg or as the 'transhuman'. Accepting that we are using technology to increase constantly the 'visible' portion of the world means also that even if the distance between the conceivable and the presentable remains unchanged, the interval between them advances in direct proportion to our technological progress, revealing uncharted territories of the newly presentable. We can register this advance without judging it to be progress or regression, without calling upon Utopia and totalisation. When this interval has moved sufficiently far away from any given position, we are transformed. Exponential change means that we are transformed ever more frequently.

Screens and manifolds

Space, as we know it, is both non-Euclidean or curved and multidimensional, containing more than three spatial dimensions. Curvature and multidimensionality are separate issues. A space can be Euclidean and four dimensional, for example, or three dimensional and non-Euclidean. Membrane theory, the present outgrowth of string theory, places the number of spatial dimensions at 11 and replaces the 'string' with the 'membrane', itself a hypersurface affectionately called a 'p-brane' (to indicate its inherent multidimensionality), as the fundamental building element.[3] In the last century, the discovery that different axiom sets produce viable alternative conceptions of space – positively curved, negatively curved or flat – created a bifurcation in the study of the nature of space. Since then, one strand is concerned with the study of physical spaces and the other strand is concerned with possible spaces; each strand subject, respectively, to empirical or logical rigour. In either case, we now think of n-dimensional manifolds. Space and surface are thus intertwined: both are manifolds, the difference between hyperspace and hypersurface being that a hypersurface of a hyperspace of (n)-dimensions is a submanifold of (n-1) dimensions. Thus the hypersurface of a hyperspace of four spatial dimensions is a space of three spatial dimensions, produced by an act of projection or section or screening.

The economies of discernment, at each level of sensing-perception-cognition-formation-creation, dictate that we come to know through a logic of selective reduction: screening. In a multitude of ways, what is known appears on or through screens that are simultaneously reductions and clarifications of worlds-at-large with which we never have direct contact. All reality, including self-knowledge, is available to us only through the mediations of screens: projections of meaning, sensory and hermeneutic filtrations, personal and political veilings. The question of the conceivable and the presentable is already a question of incommensurable screens.

To begin, there are the screens of our senses, consisting of neural arrays, synaptic nets, filters, and membranes, each receiving a narrow range of a wider spectrum, already paring off the larger portion of the raw data of the world. Then there are the cognitive screens of our interest in the world, registrations of Gibsonian affordances, themselves constrained by the lenses and filters of momentary attention. Following these are the screens of faciality, self-knowing and self-presentation. Our faces are screens, concealing and revealing identity, character and expression in double articulations of masking and becoming, veiling and viewing; so too our skin and its echoes, our clothings, architectures, avatars.

A review of literal screens would include mirrors, shadow theatres, zoetropes, cinema, television, computer monitors and the cluster of technologies pertaining to virtual reality. These are screens once removed from how we experience the world, marking the beginning of world making rather than world knowing. Here also are the psychological screens of interpersonal and social mirroring, identity formation, and political representation.

More abstract screens surround us: Stuart Kauffman's 'fitness landscapes' are the invisible hypersurfaces along which evolution and the emergence of order perambulate, climbing gradients in higher-dimensional spaces. Embedded in Minkowski's four-dimensional spacetime are three hypersurfaces defined by three kinds of 'separations': 'spacelike', 'timelike' and 'lightlike'. Two hypercones, meeting at a subjective present moment, chart out the territories of a subjective past and a subjective future. The 'lightlike hypersurface' of the cones defines all that can be reached by light emanating from the present and dictates the precise limit of causality. All that is outside the cones is the unknowable zone of indeterminate causality that is simply referred to as 'elsewhere'.

The 'spacelike hypersurface' that contains the subjective present is perpendicular to the axis of time and holds all of our familiar three-dimensional space in a conceptual but completely inaccessible universal simultaneity. That is to say, although we can conceive of a plane of pure simultaneity, no such relationship can actually exist unless the hypercones are coincident and, hence, tautological: the hypersurface screens that chart the extent of all that is in any way accessible also act as screens of exclusion of all that is 'elsewhere'.

Examining these varied manners of understanding screens, we see that they can be conceptualised into several variants: *projection* (screens proper), *protection* (screens as veils) and *selection* (screens as sieves). Screens of projection are the most familiar and are of two kinds: projections of presence (movies, television) and projections of absence (shadow theatre, shadow masks). Screens of protection include not only literal veils but all manner of costume and clothing. Screens of selection are simultaneously the most basic and the most advanced screens: at the most basic level they are articulated as the basic senses by which we detect the world within small portions of wider spectra. At the highest level they are constituted as material and conceptual technologies of sensing and effecting, enciphering and deciphering, expert systems, search engines, data mining, autonomous agents, genetic algorithms and artificial intelligences. Theories, ideologies, legal codes, value systems etc, constitute selection screens just as surely as do our senses of sight or hearing.

Transmodernity, in tracking the transformative effect of the moving interval between presentable and conceivable, is concerned also with how screens conceal even as they reveal.

Eversion: the fifth virtuality

The discussion of screens and hypersurfaces leads to questions of the nature, kinds and degrees of virtuality. We can distinguish five degrees of virtuality, as related to screens and hypersurfaces: *light and shadow*: projections of absence and presence: mirrors, shadow theatres, Plato's Cave; *sampling and statistics*: constructions of continuity from discontinuity, connotation from denotation: zoetropes, cinema, television, digital sound, transitions from discrete to continuous space and back by processes of digital-to-analogue and analogue-to-digital conversions; *inversion*: computation and epistemology, seeing through knowing, scientific visualisation, simulations, computer graphics, special effects; *immersion*: alteration, cyberspace, virtual reality, casting the world into the virtual; *eversion*: casting the virtual unto the world, multi-threading virtual/real and actual/possible.

Eversion, as the name implies, is the turning inside-out of virtuality, so that it is no longer contained in the technologies that support it but is cast into our midst and projected onto our architectures and our cities.

If screens are related to how we understand the interval between conceivable and presentable and transmodernity urges this interval forwards to the zone of transmutations and transfigurations, then everted screens become instruments by which to glimpse and enact that which is barely within perceptual or conceptual reach.

Augmented spacetime

Architecture has employed many of these screens in one way or another in its long history, but it has yet to fully comprehend and embrace screens of selection as a tectonic issue. To understand this we must register that we have entered an era in which space has lost all its innocence: we live in augmented spacetime.[4] By this I mean that space is already intelligent and imbued with nonlocality, not only theoretically but in actual practice. Technologies such as the Internet, cellular telephony, the Global Positioning System and satellite-based telecommunications have created a condition in which every point in space is activated and ready to take on different roles at any instant and for any person. Augmented spacetime is characterised by the fifth virtuality, 'eversion', but since each degree of virtuality contains the previous, all aspects of virtuality come to play in new space.

To understand this condition, it is helpful to realise that we have already constructed pockets of intelligent space on our computer monitors. A computer screen can be seen as a two-dimensional prototype of a space whose extent is fixed but whose partitions and functions change as needed or desired. This space, once confined to the user-interfaces of our computers, has already escaped the monitor and has entered the three-dimensional world at large. The language of windows, menus, icons, tools and sundry controls to which we are already habituated is being extended to the third dimension. Whereas on the two-dimensional computer screen we are embodied only as cursors and icons, in augmented spacetime we participate with our entire bodies. Just as a region of a computer monitor can take an infinite number of forms according to the software that commands it, so too can physical space adopt an infinite number of virtual architectures within the confines of a single physical space. The design of these non-retinal architectures as architecture proper is a problem we have yet to acknowledge fully, let alone master.

In the example of the computer screen as a two-dimensional prototype of augmented spacetime, the relationship between hyperspace and hypersurface becomes clear. The screen is a highly interactive, intelligent surface, a hypersurface. At first glance it has two spatial dimensions, a temporal dimension and a variety of space-related attributes such as colour, resolution and refresh rate. Its main interest, however, comes from the complex behaviours and relations it enables by being connected to the hyperspaces created by the computer that drives it and the network within which it is located.

Retinally, a two-dimensional graphical user interface will differ from the physical screen primarily on the basis of its mutability, since both physical screen and virtual interface have the same number of dimensions, while a representation of a three-dimensional real-time walkthrough will begin to depict virtual dimensions over the matrix of physical pixels, initiating the process of casting the screen into hyperspace. This process continues non-retinally, as all the behaviours of the screen are indexed into the otherwise invisible spaces of hyperlinked information and computations. The hypersurface of the screen is thus our interface to otherwise inaccessible hyperspaces. If these are not just inaccessible but also at the edge of the presentable, leaning into the inconceivable and pushing forwards, then they partake in the transmodern.

When we imagine the computer screen as a plan-view and the cursor as an avatar of our presence in an intelligent and hyperactive, transactive space, we see a premonition of the nature of our interactions, via hypersurface interfaces, with the transarchitectures of augmented spacetime. This premonition is waiting to be raised off the screen and everted into the everyday space of our embodiment.

Camera cognita
In his book *Camera Lucida*,[5] Roland Barthes, seeking the distinguishing characteristic of photography, its 'stigmatum,' explores the notion that photography records that which has been – that it is evidence that something has existed, that some event has transpired. He presses his definition further to conclude that photography articulates a double catastrophe: that something is to happen (the future implied in the photograph) that has already happened (the photograph as record of a future now past). As we know already from digital photography and special effects of all sorts, the hypersurface screens of virtuality give different testimony: to see an image is not to know that some event has transpired but that the constitutive elements of that event are known well enough to have been involved in an explicit computation. Where 'camera lucida' gives testimony to existence, the digital visual asserts a 'camera cognita' in which to see is to know. The shift from screen to hyperscreen is a shift from ontology to radical epistemology.

Within the 'camera lucida' was a screen – or hypersurface – of recording. Within the 'camera cognita' is a screen – or hypersurface – of knowing. Applying the fifth virtuality, eversion, to the third virtuality, epistemology through computation, implies turning the 'camera cognita' inside out, casting the hypersurface of knowing onto the world at large.

Transarchitectures and hypersurfaces
'Hypersurface architecture' and 'transarchitectures' are complementary concepts. While they are not identical, pursuing one soon leads to the other. Transarchitectures are permeated by hypersurfaces in both literal and metaphoric senses, and theorising and practising hypersurface architecture would lead to the radical transformations that the construct 'transarchitectures' articulates for the evolving conception of architecture.

Transarchitectures
I coined the terms 'transarchitecures', meaning the architectures of transmodernity, and 'transmodernity' in order to provide a way to discuss the overall cultural condition we find ourselves in and the overall architectural possibilities that we face. The cultural condition we witness is no longer merely modern, postmodern, poststructural, or most of the other appellations attributed to it in current discourse. Like the modern, it is a condition fully conscious of change; like the postmodern it finds all Utopias suspect, but change is now recognised as bringing forth conditions that are alien and 'trans' so that neither a romantic modern nor an ironic postmodern stance provide sufficient responses to the new problems and possibilities arising daily.

Within the overall notion of a transmodern condition, 'transarchitectures' articulates the full scope of architectural possibility at the beginning of a new millennium. In short, this is as follows: we conceive algorithmically (morphogenesis); we model numerically (rapid prototyping); we build robotically (new tectonics); we inhabit interactively (intelligent space); we telecommunicate instantly (pantopicon); we are informed immersively (liquid architectures); we socialise nonlocally (nonlocal public domain); we evert virtually (transarchitectures).

This list is doubled by the construction of an electronic, fully spatialised public domain, which is also conceived algorithmically, also modelled and simulated numerically, also built by software 'bots' and agents, inhabited interactively, used for instant telecommunication and telepresence, and within which we and our avatars are immersed in virtual spaces. These two worlds are already threaded into a new spatial continuum that, as a whole, constitutes the domain of transarchitectures. Consistent with the notion of 'transmodernity', the term transarchitectures registers this cascade of changes and points to the radical nature of the transformations facing architectural and urban theory, practice and so on, admitting, as Archigram did, that the best responses to any or all of these may soon not be recognisable as conventional architecture, but may fork into a multitude of new transdisciplines. While much of the advanced architectural debate has disengaged itself from the world that we are so fervently building, transarchitectures seek to be visionary, relevant, and open to unforeseen modes of theory and praxis. At a time when the rate of change is such that conceptual dislocation is inevitable, theorising metaphysical dislocations, while maintaining conventional practices and building wonderful but ultimately static and localised edifices, is not avant-garde, it is derivative and conservative. The links on the chain of conceptual fascinations of recent years, as potent as they promise to be, become derivative and fail to meet their promises when linked to incestuous modes of discourse, conservative modes of practice, and intolerant, reactionary and exclusive holds on power.

To a great extent, such failures are caused by the refusal by portions of the architectural theoretical establishment to acknowledge the depth of the transformation that the accelerating rate of scientific and technological advances have brought upon us – the transmodern condition – and the most radical architectural innovation of the century: the invention of virtual space in augmented spacetime.

Transarchitectures are the architectures of transmodernity in augmented spacetime, both immersive and everted.

Hypersurfaces

The cave paintings at Lascaux, Egyptian hieroglyphics, Byzantine hagiographies, Muslim calligraphies, Hendrik Willem Mesdag's panorama at The Hague, the multiple exposures in stone of the Sagrada Família, the reflective titanium skin of the Bilbao Guggenheim, cinematic projections, virtual-reality environments known as CAVEs, crystal balls and talking mirrors, and eventually, the fiction of the holodeck, all anticipate a time when surface becomes viewport, an eversion of the retina into the world, not as fantasy, but as accurate prefiguration of a condition already near at hand.

Stephen Perrella's hypersurface concept resonates with this rich history of efforts to produce depth on architectural surfaces, an effort to see surface not as an Aristotelian delimiter of space but as the portal between worlds through which subjectivity emerges. Perrella writes: 'Hyper is the existential dimension and Surface is the energy-matter substratum', parsing 'hypersurface' into an aspect of presence and an aspect of material form.[6] In his own work, this is made manifest as the culling and superposition of electronic imagery upon surfaces of differential geometry as a proposal for a concrete architecture, anticipating technologies of architectural luminescence that allow buildings to become displays, and hence, living signs. The utility of Perrella's compelling conception of hypersurface does not stop here. Akin to the notion of 'liquid architectures' but focused more closely on the built in physical space, his conception aims at the bringing together of form, presence, and information into conceptually clear formulation. Once this cluster is grasped, other ways of achieving the same consolidation are opened.

Instantiations

'Poéme Electronique', the 1958 Philips Pavilion by Le Corbusier, Xenakis, and Varése is perhaps the strongest modern precursor to transarchitectures and hypersurfaces. Integrating architecture, mathematics, music and technology, this building was formed by two surfaces: an exterior hyperbolic paraboloid similar to the one Xenakis used for his musical composition, 'Metastasis', and an interior surface likened to a 'cow's stomach'. This curious duality of mathematics and viscerality characterises the scope of the transarchitectural. Within the building, 400 speakers and a multimedia presentation consisting of projections of images from sources as varied as mythology, science, world news, art and popular culture, liquefied the space into an inhabited spectacle.

In the Cité Médiévale des Baux de Provence, in an abandoned quarry, Albert Plécy created in 1977 the 'Cathédrale d'Images', a space of subterranean projections that anticipates both transarchitecures and hypersurface architecture. Forty-six light-valves project over 2,800 slides onto 36,000 square feet of quarry surfaces every half-hour. Artists such as Hans-Walter Muller create programs of images and sounds that abduct the space and superpose a myriad other architectures upon the solid physicality of the vast quarry chambers.[7] What is most striking is how many spaces a single space can become, confounding conventional distinctions of real/virtual, actual/possible, material/immaterial. This is all accomplished using technologies that do not yet engage the computer fully, but the anticipation of the issues discussed here is unmistakably present. At some point in the program, images of architectural interiors are projected onto the quarry walls, making evident the extent of present possibility. A giant window of a Parisian apartment appears and we realise that we have come to the point of projecting onto the wall not only the image of that window but also its function. Bentham's panopticon has become what I call the 'pantopicon'. We have come to the point where we can arrange our technologies in a manner that allows us to project a virtual window where no window exists and see out of it, looking through to any place where a camera can go, or to places where cameras cannot go but computations can. The virtual window on the blind walls of the quarry can look onto the surrounding landscape, a street in Paris, the bottom of the ocean, the news on CNN, the terrain of Mars, a real-time scan of someone's brain, or into AlphaWorld on the Internet, three dimensional and inhabited by 200,000 'netizens' and their avatars.

The makers of this 'Cathédrale d'Images' belong to a generation that reached its prime before computers became ubiquitous. In the end this is a glorified slideshow, but this is no criticism, since what is presented is a clear, strong vision pertinent to the problems and possibilities we face. We can replace the slides with live video, computer animations, virtual realities; we can move out from the surface of the walls and into the volume of the quarry and make the space intelligent and interactive; we can link image and space to the Internet and to other quarries and buildings in other parts of the planet. We can take the next step, and the next, and the next.

Combining aspects of the 'Poéme Electronique' and the 'Cathédrale d'Images' with an openness to present transarchitectural possibilities, Kas Oosterhuis and Lars Spuybroek, the architects of the Janus-like Water Pavilion near Rotterdam, have begun to take such next steps. This dual building is dedicated to water, consisting of a Fresh Water Pavilion (Spuybroek) and a Salt Water Pavilion (Oosterhuis). Each in his own way, the two architects have built the first building to take mutated, augmented, transactive space as an architectural given of our times, creating an edifice in which graphics workstations are part of the architecture and real-time sensors and effectors, and interactive projections and sounds are integral to the architectural intention. Engaging the concept of 'liquid architectures' not only for its obvious proximity to the programme of a 'water pavilion' but, more importantly, as a statement of radical variability and openness to unexplored architectural potentials, they have produced the best built example of transarchitectures, a work that at once transcends categories and sets new standards for the incorporation of computation in a design. The fact that this is a dual building is important; the concept of liquid architectures is always plural and inclusive (by tolerance, not consensus), as 'transarchitectures' aims to be. The conception, design, execution and inhabitation of both parts of this building are fully transarchitectural. All of the levels of transarchitectures described above are engaged, except perhaps the last, the level of architectural nonlocality. They are already poised for breaking through this important threshold as well. The two sides of this linear building meet near the centre, at an agreed common plane, a physical section; otherwise they are quite distinct. One can imagine a pair of other planes, each one a laminar half of an interactive hypersurface encountered at the far ends of each half of the Water Pavilion, planes that become virtual portals into the other part of the building, warping the long linear space into a Möbius strip that allows people to interact with each other at opposite ends. Once in place, this short-distance nonlocality can be extended across the globe and into virtuality.

Algorithmic spectacular

As science and technology shift the conceivable, the presentable also is altered. The moving span between the conceivable and the presentable can be mined for new transarchitectural potential. In my work, this kind of mining is pursued as a research into pure tectonics. I construct mathematical models and generative procedures that are constrained by numerous variables initially unrelated to any pragmatic concerns. Even so, there are sites into which external influences can injected. Each variable or process is a 'slot' into which an external influence can be mapped, either statically or dynamically. Because the models are mathematical and algorithmic, they offer maximum compressibility – all that needs to be transmitted is the mathematical formula and the algorithm by which to unpack it, not the apparent data – and are therefore eminently suitable for transmission, either across the Internet to a virtual polis, or across the city to the office of a consultant or to a fabrication bureau.

Once the model is constructed, an iterative evolutionary process locates a set of values that fits into the variable slots and instantiates a design. These values can be derived from the particulars of the real world, from data and processes of the virtual world or from numerous techniques of capturing the real and casting it into the virtual, motion-capture, for instance. Since time is a feature of the model, if the model is fed time-based data, the form becomes animate, the architecture – liquid.

Topology does not mean curved surfaces, as the current discourse would have it, it means simply the study of those relations that remain invariant under transformations and deformations. A notion of continuity is indeed implied in this definition, but the continuity is abstract. A cube is not less topological than a blob. However, when working algorithmically, what remains invariant is the algorithm, so that a new notion of topology, 'variable topology' is introduced. While the variations in the space of the parameters and control structures that implement the algorithm may be continuous, the product of the algorithm may be to show tears and discontinuities and ever fracture into a cloud of particles or an explosion of shards. Like Raymond Roussel's method for writing, 'certain of his books',[8] the variable topology of the algorithm can take us to the alien edge of the moving transmodern presentable/conceivable interval.

My algorithmic explorations of tectonic production are concerned less with the manipulation of objects and more with the manipulation of relations, fields, higher dimensions, and eventually, the curvature of space itself. Once the architecture of objects has been set aside in favour of an architecture of relations, the notions of hyperspace and hypersurface become natural. In working with fields of force or fields of data, the notion of the isosurface is necessary; in working with hyperspaces of higher dimensions, visualisation itself requires the extraction of three-dimensional subspaces or submanifolds, which are, as mentioned above, hypersurfaces of the hyperspaces within which the designs evolve. Finally, in the case of the curved space, it is the space itself that is understood as a hypersurface that is modulated in a way that warps everything within its purview.

Typically, I compute or find a field of forces or data, scan it for isosurfaces, extrude the isosurfaces into a hyperspace of higher dimensions, transform the new higher dimensional hyperobjects in the hyperspace, project the object in a space of fewer dimensions – a hypersurface of the hyperspace – and then, finally, warp the spatial matrix itself into a new curvature of space. This elaborate process is repeated to produce alternative 'voices' to be used in a spatial polyphony. Some aspect of hypersurfaces is implicit at each step of the way, even at, but not limited to, the level of form. These forms are cast into the space of transarchitectures, the intelligent, augmented spacetime both within and outside cyberspace. This means that the design does not end with form; rather, it is the hypersurface of interface that animates the design. Each point and polygon is a known index into a body of information, placed in space and time by a known algorithm and, hence, interactive, transactive and intelligent.

The formulation of hypersurface as the 'hyper' of presence and the 'surface' of the matter/energy substratum applies, not as a description of the building-as-television, but as part of an information ecosystem of dynamically balanced constraints. Given enough computational power, connectivity and human presence, these models transform in real-time in registration with human action. In the absence of such power, or in the absence of inhabitants, they are rendered as reflective surfaces, empty virtual mirrors.

Form follows neither function nor form; rather, I am concerned with what the Situationists called the 'psychogeography' of these emergent spaces.[9] Moving from algorithmic derivations to the Debordian 'derive', from the 'naked city' to 'naked transarchitectures'. I am interested in drifting through these spaces in a condition at least momentarily uncontaminated by the spectacle. No purpose is needed; indeed to the extent that the spaces that are formed are fundamentally unfamiliar, it is possible to savour their inherent psychogeographic content in a moment of surprise just prior to the onslaught of references. Just as the invention of electronic instruments and the parallel emancipation of noise brought forth musical materials that exceeded the theoretical frameworks of their times, so too do these explorations reveal tectonic materials whose potencies and valences cannot immediately be comprehended.

Adopting pure spectacle within Debord's 'society of the spectacle' may be the only form of resistance to the omnivorousness of late-capitalist appropriation, since the imposition of any purpose instantly becomes figural and visible as a tactic or target of takeover. The alternative is to learn from the world itself: to produce an endless and unjustifiable proliferation of alien variety, within which local purposes can emerge, flourish and disappear, always pushing the very transmodern edge of (trans)evolutionary transmutation.

Notes

1   Gilles Deleuze and Félix Guattari, *Anti-Oedipus: Capitalism and Schizophrenia*, Robert Hurley, Mark Seem, Helen R Lane (trans), Viking (New York), 1977. See also *A Thousand Plateaus: Capitalism and Schizophrenia*, Brian Massumi (trans), University of Minnesota Press (Minneapolis), 1987.

2   Jean-François Lyotard, *The Postmodern Explained*, Julian Prefanis and Morgan Thomas (trans), University of Minnesota Press (Minneapolis), 1992.

3   Michael Duff, 'The Theory Formerly Known as Strings', in *Scientific American* (New York), February 1998, vol 278, no 2, pp64-69.

4   Lawrence Sklar, *Space, Time, and Spacetime*, University of California Press (Berkeley), 1977.

5   Roland Barthes, *Camera Lucida: Reflections on Photography*, Hill and Wang (New York), 1981.

6   Stephen Perrella, 'Hypersurface Infrastructure', in *Fisuras: On Interzones and Unplaces*, Banigraf (Madrid), vol 3, no 3, 1995, pp112-35.

7   François Seguret, *L'Entretien Des Illusions: Hans-Walter Muller, Claude Giverne, Xavier Juillot*, Editions de la Villette (Paris), 1997.

8   Raymond Roussel, *How I Wrote Certain of My Books and Other Writings*, Trevor Winkfield (ed), Exact Change (Boston), 1995.

9   *Theory of the Dérive and other Situationist Writings on the City*, Libero Andreotti and Zavier Costa (eds), Museu d'Art Contemporain de Barcelona, 1996.

Generative Principles for the Paracube

My ongoing investigations are aimed at arriving at architectonic propositions that are inherently liquid, algorithmic, transmissible, and derived from the geometries of higher space.

By 'liquid' I mean involving the total but rigorous variability I introduced in an essay 'Liquid Architectures in Cyberspace', and the idea that form can be driven by both data and presence, both when we are immersed in information and when information is everted on to the physical world.

By 'algorithmic' I mean both created by the algorithms and subject to a self-imposed principle of minimal manual intervention – if the results are not

acceptable, it is the algorithm, not the resultant form, that is corrected. Generally, these algorithms use artificial life and dynamic system techniques to generate or manipulate fields of data within which I discover latent forms.

By 'transmissible', I mean that since both the algorithm and the parameters of an architectonic proposition are explicitly available, the architecture is suitable for transmission to either physical fabricators or to virtual environments in cyberspace. Since what is to be transmitted is the algorithm and the parameters, or in the most efficient form, the mathematical description of the architecture, what is to be transmitted is maximally compressed.

By 'derived from higher space', I mean three things: first, employing four or more spatial dimensions; second, involving the manipulation of the curvature of the underlying matrix of space rather than the manipulation of objects; and, third, involving time as an intrinsic parameter within generative algorithms, as a dimension added to the spatial dimensions, forming a spacetime continuum.

For this project, a cuboid defined by six parametric surfaces was generated, each with its own (u,v) coordinate system. The parametric equations controlling these six surfaces were arranged in such a way as to allow variations in each surface to propagate to all the adjacent

surfaces. This, in effect, created a topological cube, a shape whose structure was inherently cubic, even though its surfaces could be made to vary dramatically by the manipulation of the equations that controlled each one.

The parameterisation also allowed the smoothness of each surface to be arbitrarily defined. Making the surfaces smoother simply meant altering a smoothness parameter. This was important in that the skeletal elements were derived from the same processes as the skin: the skin was computed at high smoothness, the skeletal structures at low.

The parametric cuboid was used to create both the structural elements and the enclosing skin of the architectonic proposition. The functions defining the parametric cuboid were manipulated to create two basic forms, one for the skin and one for the skeleton. Each of these generations involved the idea of iterative nested perturbations, an idea I adopt and adapt from computer sound synthesis, where complex timbres are constructed by adding overtone frequencies to base ones, via the inverse of a Fourier analysis, or what might be called Fourier synthesis.

The skeleton was then extruded into a fourth spatial dimension. This involved adding a fourth coordinate to three-dimensional points, adding entirely new four-dimensional points, and deriving a new four-dimensional topological structure from the given three-dimensional one. Points became lines, lines became polygons, polygons became cubes, and cubes became hypercubes or tesseracts. Once this was done, the resulting four-dimensional object was rotated about a plane in four-dimensional space by the appropriate matrix transformations. The effect of this transformation, once it was projected back into the third dimension by dropping a dimension and readjusting the topology, was that the skeleton became a space-frame. Because the extrusion into the third dimension was neither constant not linear, however, the cells of the space frame are all different, providing a rich variety of dimensions and relations.

The skin, on the other hand, was not extruded into the fourth dimension but rather was subjected to mappings that effected a curvature of the spatial matrix within which it existed. Normally, discussions of non-Euclidean geometry speak of positively and negatively curved space, but other variations are also possible. Specifically, it is possible to envision rippled spaces, spaces of varying curvature and of non-homogeneous measure. The operations on the skin used the idea of iterative, nested, timbral perturbations to create such a rippled space of varying curvature and non-homogeneous measure.

In certain studies, two skins where derived from slightly displaced sets of parameters, effecting a spatial polyphony that explored an aesthetic of varying nearnesses. This doubling of the skin happened at each of the stages described above, providing a means by which to create numerous closely-related but non-parallel geometries, each of which could then be cast into a specific architectural role, or from the interrelationship of which specific architectonic features could be derived.

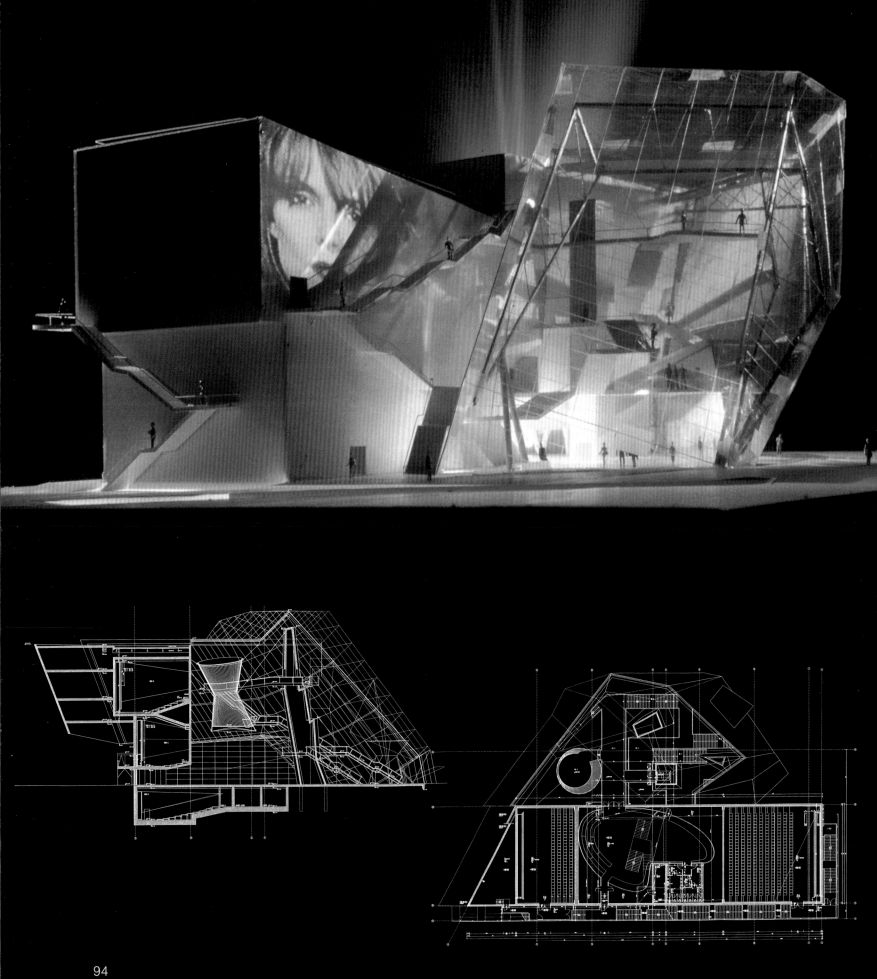

COOP HIMMELB(L)AU

UFA – CINEMA CENTRE
Dresden

This multi-purpose complex (1994-97) by Wolf Prix and Helmut Swiczinsky of Coop Himmelb(l)au, radically deterritorialises cinematic space into architectural surfaces.[1] A variety of entertainment programmes are organised, including a discothèque, five different-sized screening rooms and a lobby. In a way that is characteristic of the practice's built work, normative form is fractured and displaced in the interest of breaking the constraints of authoritarian power symbolic in the form.

This project, however, progresses beyond the group's previous deconstruction of form (most notably the Rooftop Remodelling, Vienna, 1983-89) to reconfigure relations between inside and outside; thus opening up new routes for media culture, primarily through the strategy of folding content into its structure. The effect is a significant displacement of programmatic activity which is then imbricated into the surface of a new architecture/media construct.

A form of architecture arises that questions space as merely contained or containing objects, transposing that model into 'spacetime information'. The vitality of the movie image with its ubiquitous cultural presence (weighed down with associative and iconographic meaning) is set adrift into a complex layering of transparency and opacity – a 'delay' in glass.

This condition of paused cinematic images woven into the architectural surface, generates new readings, new interpretations that release repressed, unconscious content from within the cinematic experience. Here, architecture offers itself not as a quantitative vacuum, but as an animate structure that destabilises cultural media. This activates a psychoanalytic dimension embedded within cinema: a condition that has been well described by Walter Benjamin (and more recently by art critic Rosalind Krauss in her book *The Optical Unconscious*).[2]

For Benjamin the double life of architecture is both touched and seen, whereby habits of use dominate what we see. The UFA Centre, however, reworks these sensory circuits of use and optical apprehension to create new tangibilities. Five projectors extract and re-project streams of cinematic images from the interior of the darkened theatre on to fractured architectural and glass-screen surfaces that link the cinema lobby and exterior.

By way of this inflectional strategy, the realm of cinema is resituated from its previous history of interior reflection (the pinhole camera being the prime technological example) to an interstitial zone of 'betweenness' and thus interconnection (for instance, from street to lobby to theatre).

In this work, Coop Himmelb(l)au has reconfigured architecture in order to displace cinema; the effect of which has already been anticipated in Gilles Deleuze's, *Cinema One: The Movement-Image*, and *Cinema Two: The Time-Image* (1986), in which the theorist unfolds new modalities of cinematic or haptic experience.

Stephen Perrella

Notes

1 See Tanja Widman, 'Coop Himmelb(l)au, The UFA Cinema Centre: Splinters of Light and Layers of Skin, Dresden', in *Architecture and Film*, AD Profile 112, Academy Editions (London), 1994, p48.
2 Walter Benjamin, 'Art in the Age of Mechanical Reproduction', in *Illuminations*, Schocken Press (New York), 1969, p38.

OPPOSITE, FROM ABOVE L TO R: Model perspective; section; plan

Biographies

Stephen Perrella <sp43@columbia.edu> is an architect and editor at Columbia University School of Architecture, Planning and Preservation. He is the graphic designer and editor of the GSAP's newspaper *Newsline* and managing editor of Columbia Documents of Architecture and Theory. Formerly a package designer, since 1991, he has been investigating the relationship between architecture and information. He published preliminary work in a feature article of *Wired* magazine in September 1993. He has taught architecture at various universities in the USA and has lectured internationally. He is also president of HyperSurface Systems, Inc, a design firm created to explore broader architectural interfaces for electronic technology. His associate, Rebecca L Carpenter, is an architect and graduate of Columbia University's GSAP. Perrella also collaborates with Paul Cumming and Dennis Pang, his former students. Website: www.columbia.edu/~sp43/hypersurface.html

Brian Massumi is a fellow at the Humanities Research Centre at the Australian National University. He is the author of *A User's Guide to Capitalism and Schizophrenia*, and *First and Last Emperors: The Body of the Despot and the Absolute State* (with Kenneth Dean). His book, *The Critique of Pure Feeling*, on sensation and virtuality, is forthcoming from Harvard University Press.

Michael Speaks <MAspeaks@aol.com> received his PhD in 1993 from Duke University. He has taught at the Graduate School of Design at Harvard University, Columbia University School of Architecture, Planning and Preservation, Parsons School of Design, and the Berlage Institute in Amsterdam, and is currently a lecturer in the Department of Graphic Design at the Yale School of Art. He is the editor of several books on contemporary architecture, including *Earth Moves: The Furnishing of Territories*, by Bernard Cache, and has published articles in a number of journals including *Assemblage*, *Archis*, *de Architect*, and *Daidalos*.

Gary Genosko <rariss@escape.ca> is an independent researcher, editor, and writer based in Winnipeg, Canada. His books include *Baudrillard and Signs*, *The Guattari Reader*, *Undisciplined Theory*, *Baudrillard and McLuhan: The Masters of Implosion*. He is currently preparing a manuscript entitled 'Guattari for Everyone', and editing a three volume collection *Deleuze and Guattari: Critical Assessments*.

Bernard Tschumi is Principal of Bernard Tschumi Architects, New York / Paris. He studied in Paris and at the Federal Institute of Technology (ETH), Zurich and has taught at the Architectural Association in London, the Institute for Architecture and Urban Studies in New York, Princeton University and Cooper Union. He is Chief Architect of the Parc de la Villette, won after an international competition in 1983. Currently Tschumi is Dean of the Graduate School of Architecture, Planning and Preservation at Columbia University in New York. He is a member of the College International de Philosophie, and was awarded the Grand Prix National d'Architecture in 1996. Website: www.arch.columbia.edu

Mark Burry <mburry@deakin.edu.au> is a practising architect and holds the chair in Architecture and Building at Deakin University in Australia. He is on the editorial board of the refereed journal *Exedra* and as Consultant Architect to the Temple Sagrada Família has published widely on the work of Antoni Gaudí, untangling the the architect's compositional strategies in his final years. Currently he is documenting Gaudí's Sagrada Família nave roof design for construction later this year.

Reiser + Umemoto Jesse Reiser is a fellow of the American Academy in Rome and adjunct assistant professor of architecture at Columbia University. Nanako Umemoto was formerly adjunct assistant professor of urban design at Osaka University of Art and is assistant professor of architecture at Columbia University.

Lars Spuybroek <nox@luna.nl> is an architect and one of the founders of NOX, a design office with a truly multi-disciplinary approach to architecture and design, realised in such projects as *Soft City*, a television production for VPRO TV (1993), the *NOX-A*, *-B*, *-C* and *-D* books (1992-95), *SoftSite*: a liquid city generated by behaviour on the Internet (V2_Organization, 1996) and projected on the facade of The Netherlands Architecture Institute, and the interactive water pavilion, named H_2O eXPO (for the Dutch Ministry of Transport, Public Works and Water Management, 1997). In addition to lecturing and teaching, Lars Spuybroek is also editor of the quarterly magazine *Forum*.

Kas Oosterhuis <oosterhuis@oosterhuis.nl> is founder and director of the multidisciplinary practice, Oosterhuisassociates, in which architects, artists and programmers join forces. Award-winning projects in The Netherlands include: the Salt Water Pavilion (1997) and the Garbagetransferstation Elhorst/Vloedbelt (1995). A book on the combined work of Kas Oosterhuis and visual artist Ilona Lenard was released in April (010 Publishers). Websites: www.oosterhuis.nl and www.lenard.nl.

Studio Asymptote <info@asymptote.net> Hani Rashid is associate adjunct professor of architecture at Columbia University; Lise Anne Couture is associate assistant professor of architecture at Columbia and Parsons. Their projects reveal an interest in the spatial territories inspired and made problematic by virtue of media, digital technologies, cultural blur and information proliferation. Recent works include a 30,000-square-foot multi-media theatre constructed in 1997 in Aarhus, Denmark, and a virtual architectural environment for the New York Stock Exchange. Asymptote's URL: www.asymptote-architecture.com

Bernard Cache/OBJECTILE (with interior designer Patrick Beaucé and architect Taoufik Hammoudi). As a senior consultant in image telecommunications and digital television, Cache conducted strategic studies for Philips, Canal Plus, France Telecom and France Television. He has published articles in newspapers such as *Liberation* and *Mediapouvoirs*, and is the author of *Earth Moves* (1995) and *Terre meuble* (1997), which stem from his philosophical and architectural theory; he received a diploma of the Institute of Philosophy (MBA: ESSEC) under the supervision of Gilles Deleuze. Cache has lectured extensively and taught social sciences at ESSEC and information economics at IFP. As an architect, he developed the Objectile software with TOPCAD. Website: <www.objectile.com>

Van Berkel & Bos Ben van Berkel set up in architectural practice in 1988 in Amsterdam with Caroline Bos, realising industrial projects such as the Karbouw an ACOM office buildings and the REMU electricity station; several housing projects; and interior projects such as the Aedes East gallery in Berlin. Recent work includes a new museum for the city of Nijmegen and a museum extension in Enschede, various housing and mixed-use projects and the Erasmus Bridge in Rotterdam. Van Berkel was visiting professor at Columbia University in New York, and Diploma Unit Master at the Architectural Association in London where he graduated with the AA Honours Diploma in 1987. Website: http://www.nai.nl/www_riq/RiQ_expo.html

Marcos Novak <marcos@aud.ucla.edu> is a 'transarchitect', artist, and theorist investigating the emerging tectonics of technologically-augmented space. He is the leading proponent of virtual environments as autonomous and fully architectural spaces and of the Internet as an unprecedented, non-local, transurban, public domain. His work seeks to combine non-Euclidean conceptions of space with aspects of algorithmic emergence and morphogenesis. He lectures worldwide and is Visiting Associate Professor of Architecture at UCLA (CA). Information about transarchitectures can be located on-line at – http: //www.archi.org>. Information on Marcos Novak can be found at: http://www.aud.ucla.edu/~marcos/

Claude Parent is an architect living in France. He is best known for his collaboration with Paul Virilio and Andre Bloc and for the development of the concept of the 'Oblique Function', which is seminal to the current topology emphasis in architecture.

Coop Himmelb(l)au is headed by architects Wolf D Prix and Helmut Swiczinsky, producing work that is notable for its deconstruction of form, evident in the Rooftop Remodelling, Vienna (1983-89). Among their many projects are the Biennale Pavilion, Venice (1995) and the recent UFA – Cinema Centre in Dresden (1994-97).